In God's School

In Ireland, Portugal, Angola and Zambia

Eric McCaughren

AMBASSADOR INTERNATIONAL
GREENVILLE, SOUTH CAROLINA & BELFAST, NORTHERN IRELAND

www.ambassador-international.com

In God's School
In Ireland, Portugal, Angola and Zambia

Paperback: ISBN: 978-1-64960-398-2

Printed in UK

Ambassador International
Emerald House
411 University Ridge, Suite B14
Greenville, SC 29601
www.ambassador-international.com

Ambassador Books and Media
The Mount
2 Woodstock Link
Belfast, BT6 8DD, Northern Ireland, UK
www.ambassadormedia.co.uk

Contents

INTRODUCTION

After a worthwhile and tiring busy two weeks preaching and teaching in Kuito in the southern Angolan province of Bié, my wife and I needed to return to Luanda, the capital where we were living. After a few days, we were 'booked' to fly on a United Nations flight back to Luanda. I use 'booked' in the loose sense of a mixture of probability and possibility. The believers borrowed a pickup truck and with great kindness transported us to the airport to wait for the small UN plane that was scheduled to collect us before proceeding to Luanda to land there before dark. As the believers needed to return the borrowed truck to its rightful owner, they couldn't delay by waiting with us until the plane arrived. After many warm-hearted hugs, we waved them good-bye.

The airport building was nothing like the picture most people would have of a proper airport complex. It was simply a much fought-over shell with smashed windows and no doors that close. Inside there were no seats, no toilets, no representatives of any airline. Nothing. Anything that could be carried away had long since gone. Even the concrete floor had seen much better days, but it was OK as we were just waiting a short time.

So, we listened for the sound of an approaching aeroplane. There was no control tower or any of what would be expected at even a rural African airport and of course no electricity just as there was none in the town either, except for those who could afford a generator and the fuel to run it.

The afternoon light began to give way and that is when we began to feel anxious as there were no runway lights to assist in landing. If the plane did not appear very soon then it wasn't coming. Light faded completely quite quickly as there is no prolonged twilight in the tropics so we were alone in the empty shell of an abandoned rural airport some miles outside of the town of Kuito in the province of Bié, in south-central Angola. There was virtually a night curfew as it was unwise to venture out after dark even in the middle of the town. What made it more worrisome was that we knew the UNITA opposition troops were not far away. It was too far to walk even with our small suitcases back towards the town and anyhow, after dark there was no traffic allowed to pass. So, there we were, two abandoned folk in a dangerous location with not even a seat to sit down. We had a small torch.

What added to the discomfort was the start of what was a normal tropical storm, complete with terrifyingly loud thunder accompanied by sizzling streaks of forked lightning and persistent torrential rain. We were thankful that we could move around to avoid the leaks in the roof. We prayed but with no idea how the Lord could possibly rescue us from such a situation. It seemed utterly impossible – even for the Lord?

As the evening passed and the storm continued it was hard not to come close to despair. There were only three vehicles that were intact in the whole town but none of them would be likely to even venture out at night. Armed bandits were plentiful as were guns of all types.

Imagine our amazement when we saw the headlights of a vehicle coming towards the airport building. We hoped against hope and then some. We moved from the driest part of the middle of the building to where we thought we might be more visible in the headlights. Sure enough, the vehicle came towards us. The driver flashed his lights and drew close to the curb beside what had been a door. Having noticed the large UN letters on the side of the vehicle, we didn't wait for a spoken invitation and regardless of the rain dashed towards the vehicle and jumped in. The driver expressed his amazement that we were in such a place and understandably asked a few questions. On the drive back to the town, we also asked him why he had come to the airport. He didn't really know why as he had no need to visit a derelict airport building in the middle of a tropical storm. He was an Egyptian Muslim driver for the United Nations in a UN Nissan Patrol.

He inquired where we would like to be taken and kindly left us right at the gate of the house where we had been staying. There was great rejoicing all round as they were deeply worried about us and had been praying for our safety.

Would you be surprised when I say that it was the Lord who sent a Muslim Egyptian to rescue a UK Christian missionary couple marooned in a derelict airport building that did not even have a chair of any sort and was in the middle of a torrential tropical storm? Not only so but we were in a precarious place between the two opposing sides of a civil war. Not an enviable place to be. We had no doubt that nobody else could possibly help us however much they might want to do so. Our situation was beyond normal human intervention. Then some people ask us if we are quite sure that God really answers prayer.

But to understand why my wife and I were in such an unenviable physically dangerous situation we need to go back to the beginning.

Chapter 1
IRELAND. HOLY DISCONTENTMENT

Lesson 1
Coming to know the Lord as my personal Saviour

I count it as a tremendous privilege to have been born into a home at 33 Old Ballymoney Road in Ballymena which is a small rural market town in the middle of County Antrim, one of the six counties of Northern Ireland. Both my father and mother were believers before they were married and were members of what is commonly known as assemblies of Christian Brethren. Others have called them Plymouth Brethren. I was the fourth child in the family but the first child died as a baby, as did the fifth. My brother Ronnie is 6 years older than me, my sister Mildred, 3 years older so I'm the baby.

My father, from the Ballywatermoy area in Co Antrim, came to know the Lord through the preaching of an evangelist called Mr Moneypenny. My mother, from the Gortade area of Co Londonderry, was saved through the preaching of another evangelist, Mr David Craig, often referred to as 'Scotch Davy'. She also learned that she should be baptized as a believer in Jesus Christ as her Saviour, but when the idea was mooted in her family, her older brother, Alfred resented her leaving the Presbyterian Church and joining what was commonly known then as 'the dippers' because of their practice of baptizing adult believers by immersion.

As I think both parents had already passed away, her brother Alfred had become the unofficial head of the family.

He warned her that the day she went to be baptized by 'the dippers' would be her last day in the family home and reinforced his threat by lifting down a rifle that was kept above the fireplace – a custom apparently not uncommon in country farmhouses in those days. Consequently, when she made the decision to go ahead and be baptized by David Craig in a local stream, she also packed a small case with her few belongings and was never allowed to return to her home, not even on a visit. Mr. and Mrs. Craig took her into their home on the Cullybackey Road where she helped for some time in their small home bakery and so she came to Ballymena. When my mother related that part of her past to me, I clearly understood the high importance she placed on the clear biblical teaching that a true adult believer in Jesus Christ should not be ashamed to be identified with Him by being baptized publicly.

It was ironic that many years later, in a drunken state, when trying to light a Primus stove, Uncle Alfred burnt down his shack and almost burnt himself to death. After a long spell in Magherafelt hospital, he had no home to which to return. My mother and father were kind enough to offer to take him in – on the strict condition that he would no longer drink alcohol. A condition he had little choice but to attempt to adhere to.

The irony didn't stop there. Years later when my father died in 1972 and later my mother died in 1977, my Uncle Alfred was the only one left living in our family home. After my mother's funeral, he asked me if he would have to leave. It was my pleasure to tell him that the house was at his disposal as long as he needed it. The Lord was speaking to him loudly at that time but to the best of my knowledge, he never trusted Christ.

That may have been one factor contributing to my deeply held conviction that all believers should be strict teetotallers with the exception of wine at the Breaking of Bread and even then it is often wiser to use a substitute for wine if any recovering alcoholics are members of the fellowship.

As a boy, I attended and enjoyed Sunday School in Wellington Street Gospel Hall where committed Sunday School teachers faithfully explained the way of salvation. Some really made an effort to make the Bible interesting to young minds, but all insisted that we learn at least one verse every week – and I did. That was in the King James Authorised Version.

When I was in my early years of secondary school at Ballymena Academy two evangelists had what was then commonly called 'a series of meetings' in Wellington Street Gospel Hall. I was expected to attend as my parents put a higher priority on salvation than on school homework. The preachers were Mr. Harold Spurgeon Paisley and an elderly gentleman, a retired policeman, Mr. Tom Campbell. I can still see him. He seemed old-fashioned as he wore a butterfly collar. They made quite a formidable team of totally sincere direct gospel preachers. I was already concerned that both my older brother and sister had already trusted Christ so that I was the only one in my family not saved.

School attendance was highly regarded in our family as my parents clearly valued the potential opportunities denied to them because of their lack of formal education. For that, I am deeply thankful. That's not to say that my parents didn't have a basic education. My father told me that he walked to school a long distance but carried his shoes over his shoulder until he came in sight of the school when he stopped to put them on. After school, he did the reverse on his way home. That was to save him from wearing out his shoes. There was no money for new ones.

Other than when we really were quite sick, school attendance was obligatory. So it was with some surprise that I recall my mother saying one morning that there was no need for me to attend school that day. Her spiritually perceptive mother's heart realized that I truly longed to be saved. She pointed me to various passages of Scripture, many of which I had already learned by heart in Sunday School. It was some time before she guided me to read John 3. It was clearly the Holy Spirit that enlightened my mind and opened my heart as I read verse 36 'He that believeth on the Son hath everlasting life but he that believeth not, the wrath of God abides on him.' I knew for certain that I was a sinner even though I had never done anything heinous, but I was truly sorry for my rebellious heart. I truly believed that Jesus, the Son of God, died for my sins on the Cross and I was sure of that. It was as simple as that. That was on Friday 7th November 1958. My mother was delighted though maybe just a tinge uncertain if I had really believed. My parents did all they could to encourage me.

A schoolteacher had an important impact on what God was trying to teach me. Miss Cara G. McCarroll who lived on the Ballymoney Road in Ballymena, taught French to 'A' level and also ran the after-school Bible Union. She was a dedicated member of Cullybackey Reformed Presbyterian Church. She invited good preachers and Bible teachers to speak at Bible Union, where I in due time became a Committee Member and President. She very actively encouraged us all to read our Bible daily, have a Quiet Time as she termed it, and supplied us with Scripture Union notes at her expense. She was not slow to challenge us as to what we had read in our Quiet Time so it was wise to make sure you could give an honest answer – she was just as likely to ask some well-worded follow-up questions. I thank God for this highly committed lady. It worked. I got a love for God's Word. God was teaching me to read His Word, value it and take it seriously.

Not only so, she invited overseas missionaries to come to speak to us at Bible Union but one memorable occasion stands out. She invited Gladys Aylward, 'the Small Woman' a missionary to China to come to the Academy on 17th September 1963 and persuaded the Principal Mr. W. H. Mol to allow her to speak to the whole school, both pupils and staff, in a morning assembly and she was given extra time beyond the normal. With her was a little Chinese boy from one of the orphanages she had established. She made an indelible impression about the value of dedicating our intellect and abilities to serve the Lord wherever we might go in life. She passionately exposed the evils of Chinese communism and spoke about life in Formosa (now Taiwan).

Only eternity will reveal the impact of godly teachers, whether in Primary or Secondary schools or at Tertiary level.

Lesson 2
Early influences and experiences. Learning to trust God

Sunday School at Wellington Street Gospel Hall included a class for boys of about ten 17 and 18-year-olds, most of whom were studying for 'A' levels with the hope of going to University. It was taught by Mr Hill Gaston Junior, a Maths teacher in Ballymena Academy, so I had him six days a week. He taught us not only the Scriptures but also how to ask hard questions about Scripture even tackling the book of Job. Those hard questions included asking questions about God and His ways. That study lasted quite some time but gave an interesting introductory insight into an unfamiliar book.

While still a teenager I was somehow motivated to join my brother Ronnie on the group for Open-air preaching on a Saturday evening at the corner of Bryan St and Wellington St., with older young men like Jack Law, David McNeill, Matthew McKillen, Jim and Dave McMullan, Norman Barr and Newt Beggs.

I passed my 'A' level exams and went off to university which meant long student holidays. My older brother had become interested in assisting in his short holidays with teams of GLD (Gospel Literature Distribution) in the South of Ireland. This was an excellent attempt to assist the few full-time workers in the south and west of Ireland, working alongside them and under their guidance.

My brother joined the first team in 1964 and encouraged me to do the same so I joined a team in 1965 and we were one of a few brothers on the various teams. We carried a small selection of Christian literature including the Monsignor Ronald Knox version of the New Testament. Reception at the doors varied from polite hostility to being invited in with traditional Irish hospitality. On one occasion I was heartily received by the lady of the house who produced the best fine china tea set to celebrate appropriately the first Protestant peculiarity to have reached that remote village. The whole village converged at the door and asked me good-naturedly to explain what I was about. That offered a wonderful opportunity to explain the simplicity of salvation by faith and add my own simple testimony. Lots of questions followed. Bryan Street corner had been good training seeing that some passers-by stopped to ask questions and some of them asked hard questions.

As I recall it, the origin of Gospel Literature Distribution was the result of a visionary group of spiritually alive men who wanted to assist the few full-time workers in the South of Ireland trying to spread the gospel; Dr George McDonald, a retired missionary from Congo, from Dublin's Merrion Hall; Dennis and Terry Gilpin (Bangor); their cousin Arthur Williamson (Armagh) and at the heart of it all Bert Gray (Cork). I recall that Dr McDonald's bald head held a certain fascination as he had a metal plate screwed to the top of his skull. The plate with its screws was clearly visible. It certainly didn't prejudice his Bible knowledge or keenness of intelligent observation.

GLD made an impact. God's schooling was continuing. It was an eye-opener to trudge along country lanes in the West of Ireland alongside a fellow believer from an assembly somewhat different from what I was used to. We had time to discuss and even argue over a whole range of views but had the sense to see them as of secondary importance as we worked as a team to present the gospel in a relevant way to people unaccustomed to the gospel of the grace of God through faith and not by any good works. It was also an immense privilege to learn God's Word and God's ways in the evenings from men who knew their Bible and their God – Robert McLuckie, Gilbert Stewart, Dr. David Gooding, Jim Currie – at home from Japan - and others. They joined the teams and led the evening devotions – prayer and Bible Study. These were godly men of outstanding character yet kindly and approachable. I had never had the opportunity to spend time with such men previously. They set a high standard, made a deep impression, and expected us, young fellows, to study Scripture, take it seriously, and get to know God personally. Friendships were formed that have lasted a lifetime.

As a long-termer on several teams, I became the map keeper, recording every road and house covered and also taking care of the supply of food and books as well as acting as car or minibus driver. I hadn't ever done any of that before. The Lord was graciously teaching me and helping me to develop new skills.

Several experiences stand out though apparently relatively trivial at the time. On one occasion I was returning a minibus to its owner and had offered a lift to a much older single lady who was serving the Lord also going part of that way. We went into a café for some lunch and to my surprise, the lady admitted that she had no money. I had some but not much. It was a salutary lesson that I, a seemingly penniless student, could share with a servant of the Lord. I needed to begin to see money as something for sharing to meet the needs of the Lord's work and His people and not just 'mine', little or much. It was and is the Lord's money. All of it. The schooling was ongoing.

Another very different lesson relates to an occasion when we as a team were finding it impossible to persuade anyone to even touch a single copy of the Monsignor Ronald Knox version of the New Testament that we had on offer. There was no way they were going to read any verses in it. From listening carefully to people on their doorstep, slowly we came to the conclusion that the Roman Catholic parish priest had publicly been warning his flock not to have anything to do with people calling at their doors with literature, as it was not allowed for good Roman Catholics. We prayed to ask the Lord for guidance. Eventually, it was decided that one of us should go and disillusion the parish priest. With much fear and trembling, I went to the parochial house and was greeted by the housekeeper to whom I admitted I had no prior appointment. I was very politely received. The parish priest was, I suspect, more than a little surprised to see me when I explained the reason for my visit. He carefully examined the Imprimatur of the Roman Catholic church on the front pages of the New Testament and agreed entirely that this was a good book that every good Roman Catholic could and should read. I happily gave him a copy and requested that he read it through himself and kindly recommend it to his parishioners on Sunday.

There is no way to know if he read it through, but we concluded that as good as his word, he probably did recommend it on Sunday so that on Monday and throughout that week, we had a delightfully different reception at most homes. That gave us excellent opportunities to explain the contents and share the wonderfully good news of a Saviour who finished perfectly the work of salvation on the Cross.

What a joy it was to stand on doorstep after doorstep with an open New Testament and explain simply but plainly the way of salvation by faith in Christ's finished work on Calvary. God was teaching us the need for both prayer and courage – a lesson that has needed to be repeated many times.

In a different location, there was another lesson waiting. A door was opened by a man who listened carefully to what was being said and then invited me in. It was a pleasure to explain from the New Testament the need for true repentance before God and believing faith in Jesus Christ alone. I was surprised by his reaction to a comment that all sins could be forgiven but imagine my utter astonishment when he revealed that he was guilty of killing two men – policemen. It didn't seem like it was said with any sort of bravado. He had no need to try to impress me. So it was that I relearned the need to explain the amazing wonder of God's forgiveness of a man probably also guilty of murder hanging on a cross beside the Saviour dying not for his own sins but for the sins of a criminal. Clearly, that criminal was totally forgiven by God's own Son and promised an almost immediate secure place in heaven. I pressed him to believe God's Word.

So I learned that God's justice and command for all men to repent must take precedence over society's demand for justice. I prayed with that dear man and left, pleading with him to get right with God.

I must have been a very slow learner because the Lord's ability to meet financial needs was again driven home later in a remarkable way. It came as a shock when serving as part of a GLD team in the west of Ireland when someone came from Dublin at the time third-year Trinity College Dublin exam results were posted. I had not done well I was told, having failed miserably - above all things my English Literature exam. That could mean I really had failed the year. Dr. David Gooding was leading our evening times of Bible study. He walked with me around the field where we had our caravans. Hours passed and still he encouraged trust in the Fatherly love and sovereignty of a God and Saviour who wants only our eternal best even when it makes absolutely no sense whatsoever and is painful.

There began a lifetime of a valued friendship with Dr. Gooding, in my opinion, one of the most undervalued Bible teachers in Northern Ireland. In later times when we came back to Ireland on furlough (a term now used frequently in the context of covid, but previously scarcely known) he would come to visit us for a whole day, tackle all my hard questions and feed us with a detailed exposition of Scripture, presumably whatever he had been studying and feasting on recently. What an encouraging spiritual tonic time after time. It was a privilege to talk and ask the more awkward questions that would never be mentioned in normal formal studies. Anyone who knew him won't be surprised when I say he never baulked at any question as he tried to help me grasp biblical passages that could throw some light on the answers. Like many others, I thank God for the caring, meaningful, patient input of such a spiritual giant who was unafraid of the intellectually difficult questions that sometimes troubled us. Why he ever dedicated his precious time to us I have never fathomed, but he did. Another lesson.

To some who may not be familiar with the late Dr David Gooding and his writings, he was Professor of Classics at Queen's University Belfast and a renowned international authority on the Septuagint version of the Scriptures. An outstandingly gifted expositional Bible teacher. Among a host of other achievements, together with Prof John Lennox they visited various Russian universities in the previous USSR and wrote many articles published in Russian newspapers. Their writings were circulated to libraries throughout the USSR. Information about his many books some of which are available to download is available on www.myrtlefieldhouse. com

On a hurried return to college followed by a quickly arranged interview with the Head of Department, my worst fear proved to be true. There was no misunderstanding. My mark was so low that I couldn't even be allowed to repeat that subject in November. I asked to be shown my paper and that was agreed for the following week. My confusion turned into anger as it transpired that my exam papers could not be located nor could the lecturer who graded them as he had ended his contract with the college without leaving a forwarding address. It seemed both very unjust if not incompetent and frankly beyond belief. I was clearly told that my choices were limited to leaving college permanently or repeating the year at my own expense.

My parents were not in any position to help me financially nor could I easily earn sufficient to pay a year's tuition and living expenses. I would not be in any condition to borrow money and anyhow hated the idea. My parents had instilled into me that I must save for what I wanted and never borrow money. The lender is always the master of the borrower. It's biblical (Proverbs 22:7) as well as good economic sense in every generation. I sometimes wonder if it could also be true for nations. My immediate problem was how then could I discover what the Lord wanted me to do? What was the Lord teaching me?

After much soul-searching, prayer, and Bible study I returned to the Head of Department and told him I had decided to repeat the year at my own expense. He firmly informed me when the first instalment would be due and it was soon! Could it be that I had completely missed the Lord's will and guidance after what I considered an honest year of (fairly) hard work without wasting time or resources?

Having sold the few items I possessed that were not worth much, I returned to college. One such item was my highly prized piano accordion. I never was much good at playing it but enjoyed trying. The total added up to a mere pittance. I was desperate. Money does not normally fall from heaven and yet…two days before that first instalment was due, I received an envelope in my college letter box which contained a cheque for exactly the correct amount. I paid my fees with a puzzled, bemused but very happy heart. I never did discover exactly where it came from or who sent it but was intrigued that the amount was exact. It was only very slightly less of a surprise when the same thing happened twice more. I sat and passed all my exams with my more usual moderately good grades. I never was top, but neither was I bottom.

What did the Lord mean? What was He doing in my life? What was I supposed to learn about God? Should I even ask? Maybe better simply to be thankful and push on. Put it all down to experience.

It was not easy to remain motivated to attend lectures on material I had already studied, repeating assignments, and handing them in on time. Among a group of dear Christian friends, someone mentioned that nobody seemed to be attempting to reach overseas students with respect, loving care, and a clear explanation of the gospel. Should 'we' be doing something about it? That 'we' was annoying. Anyhow, it seemed to me that God had somehow let me down badly as well as nearly miraculously meeting my financial need. I was confused. Can you understand when I say that I wasn't really on the best of terms with God just then?

In college, the plan was made to arrange a series of functions specifically for the benefit of overseas students but how could we tell how many there were and how many different nationalities? In the end, the college authorities were helpful when we explained that we wanted to put on a special evening for each main overseas nationality represented in the college with their national traditional music, food, and costumes. Nobody else was doing it. How could we ever fund it ourselves? It was fun getting access to embassies in Dublin and persuading them to help fund an evening for 'their' students whom they would get to know better and it would help if they could supply all kinds of local national costumes and instruments as well as their typical food. Amazingly, most did it.

Attendance also was amazing. I was part of that team of students committed to getting to know and support overseas students. We had to explain to them who we were and why we did it – that's the good news. We made friends who led us to their friends. Some among them were already believers who had no idea how to find other believers. God was at work. Somehow, attending repeated lectures became a lot easier. It was making sense. Could it possibly be that I was meant to have some extra time without neglecting my studies? Oh, and the Lord wonderfully met all the considerable expenses for this outreach to overseas students. We were all cash-strapped students. Could the Lord God possibly really be trusted? Or doubted?

Lesson 3
Becoming a schoolteacher. Out of my comfort zone.

I graduated from Trinity College Dublin with a BA degree in June 1969 followed by a one-year course at Queen's University Belfast to gain what was then called a Dip Ed – a Diploma in Education. I was in the privileged position of being the first in our family to graduate with a university degree.

As part of that Dip. Ed. course, we had to choose three sessions of teaching practice in different kinds of schools. I chose to teach in a Roman Catholic Primary School in

Ballymena. The Principal was intrigued by my request. He was honest enough to warn me that several members of staff might not be too impressed with my presence, but he personally was entirely sympathetic even accommodating me, a Protestant, by excusing me from participating in the morning religious assembly. That was fine with me as I had a few extra minutes in bed. That is until he phoned one morning to ask if I could come in at the normal earlier time. I agreed at once as he was a pleasant man and I liked him. Due to teacher absences, there was no one to take one Religious Education class, so would I be willing to help? Sure, but with some trepidation. I questioned my ability to teach a class of children from a Roman Catholic background without causing the headmaster and the school any embarrassment. He smiled and asked, 'Do you go to the Gospel Hall?' 'Yes' I replied. 'Then you know your Bible. Tell the children what the Bible teaches and you can't go wrong'. I admired his confidence. It turned out to be many lessons.

So, I did as requested and the very well-behaved children seemed to love the Bible stories that I knew by heart. They were lovely children. But I had another problem. How could I lead the children in the traditional 'Hail Mary, mother of God' prayer when I profoundly disagreed with the theology? Mary is never described in the Bible as the mother of God but as the mother of Jesus. He suggested that I quietly go to the back of the classroom and simply say 'Now let me hear you pray'. I considered that an excellent compromise. He was a gracious man. I suspect I learned more than the children. It was a good experience. I was still learning.

That was followed later by some weeks in Coleraine Inst., a highly respected academic Grammar School. I enjoyed it thoroughly, largely because of the kindness of the staff. My third choice was in Cullybackey Secondary School, not far from my home. There were two vacancies coming up.

I applied. It was an intimidating experience waiting in the staffroom on interview night with about thirty hopefuls. Many seemed evidently very capable and super-confident that they would get the job. I was appointed.

It was amazing to be greeted after school one day by the caretaker's question 'How are your mother and father?' It was not only asked very politely but clearly with the impression that he not only knew them but also that he knew exactly who I was. And he did. We became good friends. He was a lovely believer who took a pride in keeping the school floors highly polished. He clearly did his job 'as to the Lord'. He knew many of the children by name. It was a wonderful school for my first job.

The Vice-Principal, Stanley Johnson (recently deceased) had what you might call 'a special touch'. Once when a lad was misbehaving in the corridor, he was pulled firmly to one side by Mr. Johnson and told that if he didn't behave, he (the VP) would speak to the lad's uncle at the weekend and he would get 'what for'. It worked a treat. Local knowledge. He knew the parents and relatives of most of the children and the children knew that too. Discipline was not a problem. Uncles could punish more effectively than teachers. Mr. Johnson knew and loved the children but expected their respect – another lesson.

Lesson 4
Is there such a thing as holy discontentment?

I returned to attending Wellington Street Gospel Hall where I was a member. Looking back, it was an amazing privilege to be part of a thriving group of young post-World War 2 baby boomers who knew the Lord and wanted to serve him. With the agreement of the elders, a Sunday afternoon Bible Class was started for young people in what was then known as 'the gallery' in Wellington Street Gospel Hall. After some time, it was helped by the keenness and contagious enthusiasm of Nat Rodgers and the trusted leadership of Theo Hewitt, a missionary to Norway at home on furlough. There may have been 15-20 of us in more or less the same age group. We were free to study thoroughly and thrash out what we really believed the Bible was saying. That group formed a strong bond and later many would work happily together in various forms of outreach. They were good times. God was teaching us His will through His divinely inspired Word.

When available, visiting Bible teachers were invited. That included the ageing missionary to central Africa, Tom Rea. I recall he asked what time we started and then added 'what time does the singing end?' He was an elderly gentleman needing his Sunday afternoon rest before speaking at the evening meeting as well. He had translated the whole Bible into Lunda, an African tribal language. He opened his Bible, read the passage, then set his small Bible face down on his knee and expounded the whole passage verse by verse without so much as glancing back at his Bible. Along with many of us, I longed to know the Bible like that. He not only knew his Bible, he knew the Lord. What a privilege to have known and listened to such a godly man.

As the Scriptures got hold of us, we realised that we were taking in but not reaching out. Few so-called 'outsiders' were coming to the Sunday evening Gospel Meeting though the preaching was mostly good by well-chosen capable preachers. We started to feel what might be termed 'holy discontentment'. The streets had loads of young people roaming about with little to do but they were not coming into the Gospel Hall. Many of the 'gallery Bible class' young people started to form a 'fishing team' by going out in pairs to engage young people in conversation and invite them to come to the Sunday evening gospel meeting in the Gospel

Hall. It didn't work. The few who ventured felt totally like a trout up a tree. Neither the young lads nor the girls who came felt comfortable as they didn't wear the expected formal clothes. We slowly came to understand that.

So, we studied and prayed. The idea was conceived in 1969 of opening a Christian coffee bar. We called it 'Oasis' where young people could come in and feel at ease. We hoped and prayed that it would be a spiritual oasis. The elders applauded the idea and had enough confidence in us but would not become involved nor provide any money. A suitable empty property in an ideal location on Broughshane Street in Ballymena was spotted. It was owned by the Ballymena Development Commission who were waiting to have it demolished to allow construction of a new ring road - which incidentally never has been built.

When approached they agreed to let the house temporarily but at far too high a rent for us. We came together and had a novel idea. We chose a treasurer. Each person wrote anonymously on a piece of paper how much we could commit to paying monthly and the total was revealed. Some of us were students, some starting a first job and none were flush with money. Another approach to the council was arranged with a clear explanation of who we were and what we wanted to do with the property. They asked for time to discuss before arriving at their considered decision. The amount asked for was £25.00 which matched perfectly what we could commit to, but of course, they didn't know that. We took it as God's overruling. Another lesson.

The house had many rooms, but all were empty. The word went out. Older fellow believers furnished the place with unneeded but still good furniture. Alterations were made, a wall was knocked down and a steel beam was put in place to make a large ground-floor room. That elderly uncle of mine was a carpenter. Though totally opposed to the gospel he made many medium-sized tables. We fitted it out with piped [Christian] music into every room from my reel-to-reel long-playing Sony tape recorder. The kitchen provided tea, coffee and biscuits free of charge. Each Saturday and Sunday evening we first met for prayer then divided the team into two – the 'fishers' and the 'stayers'. Fishers went out two by two into the streets, fellows together, girls together. The stayers were allocated two by two to the various rooms with different activities, board games, table tennis, etc. It is always easy to organize willing workers who want to serve the Lord.

A 'bouncer' was needed. A well-built local butcher, Wilbert McMullan, a lovely very kind gentle godly man, an older man with some 'gravitas' was roped in. He did an excellent job and being older than the rest of the team also helped. He was a vital member of our team. No drunks were allowed in but were kindly invited to come back the following week when sober. The place was soon humming with young people many of whom had no church connection. At a set time all were called to the main large room and they all came without any fuss. A varied programme was arranged- 'Fact and Faith' 35 mm films, testimonies – including a policeman from our assembly. Invited speakers were varied and included Dr. Gooding. It needed a certain skill to communicate the gospel to such an audience and be unafraid of interruptions and good questions. The amazing thing is that we gained the respect of the young people so that none of them gave us any serious trouble. A few professed faith in Christ as their Saviour but many heard the gospel in an informal atmosphere probably for the first time. Some are going on strongly for the Lord to this day. The house was often full and continued for several years.

Younger people were encouraged to come alongside some of us slightly older ones. A younger man called Thomas Wallace tells how he was paired with Alan Clarke at the same table. Alan asked him to tell the young people how he came to know the Lord and how they could do the same. He was flabbergasted but says he went home realising he needed to read his Bible seriously and get to know it. He did and the Lord has used him wonderfully as a gifted evangelist.

Sometimes I think that we young people learned so much from the Lord through those many varied experiences and how to present the gospel to those unaccustomed to hearing it, lessons that have been a real lasting blessing throughout our lives. There seems to me to be no substitute for young people getting their sleeves rolled up and following the Lord's prompting to serve Him in their own town or city. Once a young believer gets a taste of witnessing to unbelievers by explaining the gospel simply, it is hard not to want to continue. The Lord was so good and gracious to us all despite our inexperience, but we were learning the value of believing prayer. We prayed together before every activity and fully expected the Lord to answer. He did and He still does.

We were grateful for the Lord's preserving care as the police opened a competing 'Blue Light' disco very close to where we were but had to close it down as they failed to keep order and the place was wrecked.

Lesson 5
Dunclug Gospel Hall. New training.

Redevelopment of part of Ballymena town centre led to a plan to relocate the Wellington Street assembly to another part of town. The Tower Shopping Centre was built on the vacated land. A site was found in Cambridge Avenue to which the assembly relocated in 1974, but the elders were also persuaded to buy an ample site near a new housing development on the Doury Road at the other end of town where they also agreed to fund entirely the construction of a new temporary building which was completed in 1978. Many were enthusiastic about that vision. It was known as Dunclug Gospel Hall. With much prayer, children's work began in the summer of 1978 and the work developed.

There was weekly door-to-door visitation informing people of who we were, where we came from, and what the Bible teaches; the new building was clearly visible on the side of the hill on the way into the new housing development. At one door there was a mixture of curiosity and scepticism. I was invited in.

That initial visit led to the family agreeing to a weekly Bible Study which was based on the Gospel of John and gave an opportunity to clearly explain the gospel and answer lots of questions. The result after quite some time was that the couple trusted Christ and their children attended the Sunday School and other meetings for young people. They had never been married but came to understand that their past behaviour could be forgiven but also needed to be rectified. They were married in a civil ceremony with the active encouragement of the leadership at Dunclug Gospel Hall. Over time several of their children professed faith.

As the number of neighbours and friends attending that weekly home Bible Study increased, the living room became uncomfortably full. That was remedied when a couple attending suggested having a Bible study in their home, and a second group was formed but it never thrived like the first one. Others professed faith in Christ, including some with a variety of personal and social problems.

In ongoing harmonious prayerful consultation, our deeply respected elders at Cambridge Avenue graciously agreed that it was an opportune time to start a new assembly. They also very kindly sent a letter to local assemblies and at least two circulation magazines giving the information that the first Breaking of Bread would be held on Sunday 7th October 1979 in full fellowship with the Cambridge Ave assembly. It was another lesson and a hard one when sadly some believers spread the false information that no such letter existed or was ever sent. Many years later that fellowship of local believers became Hillside Community Church.

For some time, the work continued at Dunclug Gospel Hall under the temporary guidance of an unofficial leadership of those men most enthusiastically involved and committed to the work. As time went past it was felt that a more organized biblical eldership should be recognized but this was a new experience for us all as the elders at Cambridge Avenue didn't offer to be involved in that process even though we had hoped that several of them might wish to join us and give some guidance and direction. We were very grateful to Nat Thompson, father of Jenny Rodgers, who was an older more mature believer for his wisdom, experience, support and assistance. In 2020 he celebrated his 100th birthday and since then has passed into the presence of His Lord.

We studied together 1 Timothy 3 and Titus 1. What we did first, therefore, was to ask all the members to think prayerfully in light of the biblical required characteristics about whom they recognized as their 'elders' and then anonymously write down the names on a sheet of paper. They did so. When all the replies were submitted it became obvious that certain names occurred the most frequently, so we took it that the Lord had guided in the whole process and those men were recognised publicly as 'elders' though several of us were relatively young. They were Nat Thompson, Dr. Donald Gaston, Nat Rodgers, Alan Clarke, and myself. With considerable fear and trembling, we undertook the responsibility. We comforted ourselves in that we gathered that several of the Lord's early disciples were also quite young, though there the analogy clearly ended. There developed a firm trust and friendship between us as elders and especially those of us who were nearly the same age. They were very busy but thoroughly enjoyable days as we saw the Lord blessing our vision and hard work. We were learning a little more.

Nat and Jennifer Rodgers were a vital part of that initial leadership team. Their infectious enthusiasm and godly character made them indispensable. Not only quite rightly had Nat Rodgers been recognised as an 'elder' in the Dunclug assembly but in their spiritual journey, they became convinced that the Lord wanted them to serve Him abroad. Over some years they had been in regular touch with Theo and Margaret Hewitt who were serving the Lord in Norway. Eventually, in 1982 they were commended to full-time service as missionaries in Norway initially working alongside Theo and Margaret.

Lesson 6:
A lovely godly young lady.

On one occasion I was based with a sizeable Gospel Literature Distribution team in Merrion Hall in Dublin. My older brother Ronnie was there on his holidays from work in the Belfast aircraft factory of Short Bros and Harland. We were the only pair of brothers on that team. Those were memorable days as we trudged Dublin's streets and sometimes slept less than was desirable as Derek Bingham and Sam Patterson and others kept us royally entertained when we should have been asleep. Derek's superbly accurate mimicking of a wide range of gospel preachers was hilarious – Ian Paisley, Harold Paisley, Hedley Murphy, and many others - so how could anyone sleep?

As mentioned earlier I had many happy times working with GLD teams in S. Ireland in a variety of capacities as I often spent most of the summer months helping where I was deemed useful. On one occasion the loaned minibus I was driving was needed to transport young campers from Cork to a Postal Bible School Camp at Beltra in County Sligo. It was a long tiresome drive along winding cross-country roads with a full minibus load of young people not all of whom were good travellers. Need I say more? So, when I arrived very late at night at Beltra neither they nor I were at our best but were greeted by a lovely young lady who was nothing but kind and understanding. She was Margaret Stewart. Very tired, I rolled into a camp bed in a tent shared with George Hall, the camp speaker. Early the next morning I had to be up and away but not without a good breakfast.

On one such team based in Merrion Hall, Margaret had volunteered to help Jean Giff and Betty Mahood in the Postal Sunday School office in Merrion Hall to free Betty to help with girls' camps in the west of Ireland. She was also only too willing to help with the catering needs of the GLD teams. It didn't take long to discover that she was from the North, a teacher and needing a lift back to Northern Ireland and I had an empty car. How fortunate was that? The Lord moves in mysterious ways.

She was a teacher in Magherafelt Technical College but had just secured a teaching post in Cambridge House Girls School in Ballymena teaching Chemistry and Biology. Both she and her younger sister Irene were not too hard to coax to visit Ballymena and help with the work among young people in Oasis. Both sisters played the piano – always a useful and much-needed asset, of course.

With both of us based in Ballymena, deeply interested and involved in the same work among young people, the attraction grew steadily as our friendship deepened. It soon became obvious that the Lord had brought us together and that we were ready and happy to spend our lives together doing whatever the Lord wanted us to do and wherever that might be.

We were married on the 7th July 1972 in what was then Wellington Street Gospel Hall. It was demolished in preparation for the building of the Tower Shopping Centre. We sometimes joke that we were married in front of Boots' camera counter. Well somewhere like that.

Chapter 2
A VISIT TO ANGOLA

Lesson 1
Would visas be granted?

My father was brought up in the townland of Ballywatermoy outside Ballymena and became friends with a neighbouring young man called George Wiseman who decided to emigrate to the USA. There he came in contact with believers and married an American young lady. They answered the call of the Lord to serve as missionaries in Portuguese-speaking Angola. Every so often George and Emma would visit friends back in Northern Ireland including my parents.

As I was growing up there were many memorable times when I listened enthralled to George's exciting stories about life in Angola and especially his missionary itineraries to a remote area of Angola called Camaxilo. Those stories included snakes – big snakes, deadly snakes, scorpions, hippos, and lions. Such stories enthralled me as a boy but at the same time opened my eyes to what the Lord was doing overseas, widening my horizons.

George was a crack shot with a rifle, apparently a skill learned in his youth enabling him regularly to win prizes for shooting at country fairs. That skill was well utilized in Angola where villagers terrorized by lions or hippos would come asking him to go and shoot the marauding dangerous animal. That of course made him very welcome and at the same time opened the door to explain the gospel.

He loved sitting around the evening village campfire talking about the good news of the gospel and the Lord's gracious salvation. He was widely used by the Lord as a gifted evangelist to see many come to know the Lord. Over many years George visited Camaxilo with other missionary colleagues including Crawford Allison, David Long, Willie Hastings, and Roy Wood. The story of that work is utterly amazing, a work of the Holy Spirit. George was one of the most self-effacing genuinely humble men that I have ever met and never boasted of his role in that work but constantly gave credit to the work of the Holy Spirit. What is most amazing is the way in which the Lord first used Angolan evangelists who initiated the work in that part of Angola before any foreign missionaries visited that area.

The story is fascinating. I recall hearing George speak about it. Men were forcefully taken from Angola to work on plantations on the island of São Tomé where they heard the gospel clearly preached by other Angolans who had earlier likewise been taken as virtual slaves to the island. Then when they eventually were allowed to return to Angola they fearlessly preached the gospel. I take the liberty to quote from what Ernest Wilson wrote in his book 'Angola Beloved' where he quoted from a letter published in Echoes of Service missionary magazine (still published monthly) of how an entirely indigenous work developed without any missionary input.

It was started by two Africans, Francisco and Muido. The latter is Chokwe from Saurimo, taught by Mr. Allison. Francisco is Lu-unda man who was sent on contract labour to the island San Tome, where he heard the gospel and was converted through the work of ...Africans. He was a John-the-Baptist type, completely fearless and a tireless evangelist.

Robert Allison, in a letter dated August 1957 to the missionary magazine, Echoes of Service, described a visit to Camashilu with George Wiseman:

"Mr. Wiseman and I have just returned from the Shinji country again and what we witnessed this time was something to be seen to be believed. We had heard some stories of a great spiritual upheaval going on among them. Our faith was small indeed. At our first meeting in Camashilu proper there were approximately 500 listening to the gospel and we were amazed at the good number and interest.

"'But,' said the believers, 'the people have not come yet.' In the morning at 6 o'clock, 1,000 were there waiting for us to get out of our camp beds for the gospel meeting. All that day they kept streaming in to the encampment— men, women, and children. "That evening there were 2,000 people, and the following morning at 6:00 o'clock, when we went down to the river for some to be baptized, the place seemed black with people, fully 2,000 strong.

So when the white missionaries arrived, the people were amazed that the message was the same as they had heard from their own evangelists who had returned from São Tomé, and somehow, in an exceptional manner the Holy Spirit had prepared that area to receive the gospel so that many thousands turned to Christ for salvation. It was reported that the elders baptizing the new converts in the river had to continue all day so numerous were the new believers. I remember seeing photographs of long lines of believers waiting in an orderly fashion to be baptized.

It was only when we accompanied George and his wife to visit Camaxilo on a later occasion that we got a glimpse of the many, many assemblies that had been planted in that area over the years and some of them were large with several hundred believers. George had a high regard for one of the early Angolan evangelists whom we met, an elderly frail man with whom he had a great reunion.

But I get ahead of myself. Back in Ballymena, Margaret and I became increasingly involved in helping the Wisemans by locating and shipping supplies; supplies that were unobtainable in Angola despite it being a very wealthy oil-rich country that was being ruined by civil war. Air freight was the only reliable way to ship supplies. It was expensive but we were earning good salaries. I recall delivering some goods to the cargo section of Aldergrove airport where the official who was helping us came back with the bill. He indicated that it might be advisable to sit down before he mentioned the freight cost. It was a privilege to be allowed to assist.

George's American wife Emma passed away and was buried in a cemetery in Harare, Zimbabwe. He later married Ena Bell who had worked alongside them as a nurse in the clinic at Biula. On a visit to our home, George and Ena invited us to consider visiting them in Angola, at Biula Mission Station. George knowingly pointed out that we were teachers with a two-month long summer holiday. We prayed about it and decided to take up the suggestion, but totally aware that Angola had a post-independence pro-Russian communist government not at all friendly to Christian missionaries. We had to apply for a Visitor's Visa for each of us. If either one was granted but the other refused we would deem that a refusal. We learned that such a discouraging tactic by those in the government department was not uncommon. The likelihood of both of us receiving Visitor Visas seemed severely diminished when a Christian friend whom we knew was refused.

We applied, knowing that both Visas needed to be for June and July when we had school holidays. May or September would be no use. We asked the Lord to kindly overrule even in the Angolan communist bureaucracy if it should be His will. Both Visas were granted and we were notified on 28th May 1982 – yes and for the correct timespan. Our reading that day was Ruth 3:18 which encouraged us even though taken somewhat out of context. It read 'the man will not rest until he has settled it today'. You can see how the Lord was gently encouraging us to trust Him. We were amazed but happy that the Lord was opening the doors in ways we couldn't possibly influence, except by prayer.

Of course, we were unaware of just how ideal were the months of July and August for visiting Angola. It was in the dry season which lasts from May to September. The wet season starts usually towards the end of October and continues until April. Nor did we know that Biula Mission Station in Moxico (pronounced Mosh-iko) Province where we were headed was also on a high plateau.

Those interested in geography will know that Angola is a huge country more than five times the area of the UK, lying south of the 12th parallel, bordered on the north and northeast by the Democratic Republic of Congo, Namibia to the south, and Zambia to the southeast. It is a steep climb from the coastal plain onto the high plateau.

As for temperature, the northern part of Angola is hot, tropical with high humidity with some rainfall at the coast whereas farther south it is more temperate partly due to the cooling influence of the cold Benguela current offshore and also the 1,500-foot altitude of the high plateau. The Bié plateau is both fertile for agriculture and a very pleasant place to live and work.

The ascent inland by road from the coastal plain means a steep tortuous climb up into the plateau. It makes for some interesting driving, provided you have a reliable vehicle. If you are going in the opposite direction your vehicle needs to have good brakes and you quietly hope and pray that so too do the sometimes-overloaded trucks whose drivers may well have enjoyed rather too much cooling beer with their lunch.

The end of the dry season is characterized everywhere by large-scale but carefully controlled bush fires that burn up the grass leaving the living trees largely unscathed. That makes for one of the many unforgettable smells of central Africa.

As we prepared to book our tickets, imagine our delight when we discovered that a young English lady from Cornwall called Ruth Hadley, another schoolteacher, was also planning to travel to Angola, so we coordinated our dates. She was also going for the first time but to remain permanently as a missionary whereas we were planning only to visit. An additional bonus was that she had already been to Portugal to learn Portuguese whereas our Portuguese was very close to non-existent after only a few lessons with a young man nicknamed 'Jaffa'.

Few western airlines flew to Angola, so we booked with Aeroflot, the Russian airline, not then widely known for comfort or efficiency. We left Belfast on 5th July 1982 flying to London then onwards through Moscow and Budapest. At Budapest we had to disembark by walking carefully without the slightest hint of deviation between two rather narrow continuous lines of security officers with lots of Alsatian guard dogs. Not the friendliest of welcomes. It was the same to re-board the aircraft. I wonder where they thought we might want to escape to.

Meanwhile back in Ballymena, there was consternation on the part of our friends who knew our travel arrangements when news broke that an Aeroflot flight from London to Moscow had come down disastrously on landing with the suspected loss of all on board. Our friend Robert Moore checked with Kathleen Davidson of Greer's Travel. It would appear that the disaster took place soon after our flight landed safely in Moscow as we were totally unaware and unaffected by it. The runway was operating normally. It took some time for Kathleen to discover the truth and reassure our friends.

We made it safely to Luanda where we were met by Charlie Shorten (a Canadian missionary, died Sept 2020 aged 102) who with his American wife Betty (died Dec 2020 aged 93) cared for us right royally, but it was an education in the realities of a communist system. Everyone was supposed to have a card that permitted them to buy in certain designated shops which incidentally had almost no goods. Local 'free' markets were more or less illegal but essential for people to survive. They had only a very limited smattering of some fruit and vegetables grown locally on small plots. From the windows of the 7th floor flat we observed horrified as long lines of people queued at a hatch for bread available only on certain days. The queue was kept in line by men wielding flexible hose pipes which they were not slow to use. Some believers baked bread in their Portuguese-style burnt-brick ovens. They generously shared with the Shortens and their visitors.

There was a special proper small shop called Anglo-Diplo in which foreign diplomats could purchase what was available, but only with foreign currency, mostly United States Dollars. The dollars had to be lodged in a certain bank a long time in advance. A visit to Anglo-Diplo was another eye-opener. Shelves would have a whole row of the same item and large empty spaces with very little variety in total. Prices were something else. I recall Charlie buying three or was it four electric smoothing irons, much to my surprise. How many smoothing irons does a man need? He explained that none of his Angolan Christian friends would have access to such imported goods nor could they afford them. Even in that diplomatic shop, an electric iron might not appear again for a long time - maybe years. He was generous in helping Angolan fellow believers. Another lesson.

Purchasing tickets to fly inland to Saurimo on 14th July on the Angolan airline TAAG [Transportadora Aérea AnGolana - lovingly interpreted as Think Again About Going] was also something else. Charlie and I queued at the airline desk tightly squeezed in a scrum of Angolans. They knew nothing about an orderly English-style queue. When no more could get into the office, late arrivals simply walked on our shoulders with their over-filled suitcases to reach the front. I really feared that when Charlie and I reached the desk his ribs would be cracked against the metal counter. I had to keep behind him pushing backward with all my might to lessen the pressure on him. This was no place for the weak in body or mind. Of course, unknown to me, having a fully paid ticket was no guarantee that you would get on a flight. Tickets were sold more or less while there were people willing to buy. To actually get on, often meant paying 'a little extra'. Otherwise, you could come back another day and another day – for many days.

When we eventually arrived in Saurimo we were delighted to be met by George and Ena Wiseman who had traveled some 4 hours/ 120 klms to Saurimo to meet us. We stayed in a former missionary house on an old mission station at Camundambala, some 10 klms outside Saurimo. That house is presently very nicely repaired and occupied by Brian and Debbie Howden, a long-term missionary couple from England. It had been abandoned for many years so of course had no running water, electricity or ceilings but had lots of bugs and even a 4-foot high (1 metre +) anthill mound up through the floor in the middle of the lounge. An unusual special feature. In the past water had been supplied from a fairly clean stream pumped to the house by a hydraulic ram but by then it had to be carried in containers, calabashes, on the heads of local women. At night furry-tailed mice ran races on the rafters, so sleeping under mosquito nets has always had more value than just deterring mosquitoes. The bath served only to store water so please ask no questions about having a bath.

I recall being surprised to see the bright colour of an electricity cable stretched along a rafter but then it moved. A very dangerous snake. The Lord had graciously preserved me.

We needed to wait for Ruth's not inconsiderable luggage to arrive on a cargo plane. She would have to set up house without access to any kind of shop worth the name until she might return to the UK after two or three years. As the wait continued day after day, the food supply for five people brought by Ena from Biula Mission Station was running low. None was available locally. It had all come from parcels sent out by ladies in missionary classes, mostly in N. Ireland. Ena pointed out that it would be necessary to retrace their steps the approximately four-hour journey back to Biula - and fuel was scarce. That would have meant traveling on a Sunday. I confess we thought George somewhat stubborn for insisting that he would not travel on a Sunday. So, on Sunday we ate the few remaining scones knowing that there was no more food. A new experience.

On Monday we paid close attention to any overhead sound that might be a hint of an approaching plane before eventually George and I traveled hopefully to the airport at Saurimo and discovered that a cargo plane was indeed expected that day but with no idea what it carried. What a relief. On it were all of Ruth's luggage and three barrels of ours, two of which were 200 litre metal drums containing lots of food and also a replacement fuel pump for George's vehicle. It didn't take long to open barrels and enjoy the new food supply nor long for George and me to fit the new fuel pump ready to travel to Biula. To our consternation, we hadn't travelled very far until the newly fitted pump failed. Though new, it was faulty. A helpful assistant in Clarke's garage on the Ballymoney Road in Ballymena had gone to considerable trouble to get it sent from a remote part of Scotland as a special favour to George Wiseman for whom he had a deep respect. He couldn't know that it too was faulty.

There followed another African survival lesson – never throw away an old part until you are completely sure the new one works properly. George had brought the old one, carefully wrapped in a cloth to avoid rattles, beneath the driver's seat. He didn't like any rattles in his vehicle. By the roadside we removed the new fuel pump and replaced the old one which, mercifully, still worked a sort of a way.

The new experiences continued at Biula. On the first Sunday, the arrival of three white visitors caused quite a stir. In true African style, a welcome party came to meet us as we walked towards the hall for the Breaking of Bread. To the horror of Margaret and me, some of them had severely deformed hands and faces, even looking quite grotesque. Should we shake hands and risk serious leprosy infection or seem totally uncaringly unchristian in our first encounter? First impressions matter. I decided to follow George's example and to my amazement, he shook hands heartily. Only afterward did I discover that these were patients who had already been treated in the nearby clinic so their leprosy was no longer infectious. That was not so for many others. In the Breaking of Bread, much to my relief, there was one section of the hall reserved for leprosy patients still being treated who were served bread and red-coloured juice separately. It was a large hall seating more than 200 - African style. Of course, now leprosy is a much rarer disease as modern medical progress has provided excellent treatment.

It was at Biula that we first heard lions roar in the wild, in a nearby valley. Unforgettable. The house at Biula was not exactly luxurious. Windows frames were past their best, a fact not lost on us when one morning when we went outside, there in the dirt were the pawprints of two lions. They had circled the house only a metre from those windows. They didn't roar nor had we smelt them for they do smell, not being accustomed to using shampoo, but they may have smelt what would have made a good meal. Those fragile window frames? We were thankful for the Lord's protection.

Many years later during the ceasefire in 1992 in preparation for United Nations supervised elections when the Wisemans came on a visit, George was keen that we also visit some places away from the Mission Station. He arranged for us to make one such trip to visit some assemblies in what was a politically and militarily contested area. By that is meant an area contested between the MPLA Marxist government installed with the help of about 10,000 Cuban soldiers 'assisted' by many Russian 'advisers' back in post-Independence from Portugal in 1975 but ruthlessly opposed by the UNITA movement ostensibly fighting for free democratic elections. It was an interesting lesson in the exercise of missionary diplomacy.

When we arrived in a large village, we presented ourselves first to the office of the government officials, greeting them and explaining who we were and why we were visiting. The process of 'greeting' is vital in African society. Next was a visit a short distance away to the officials of the UNITA opposition movement, likewise transmitting our greetings and explaining the reason for our visit to them. We were politely received in both offices I suspect partly because both sides had benefitted from the medical help offered without questions at the basic medical clinic at Biula Mission station.

To my surprise, the UNITA officials insisted that we accept that two armed soldiers should attend our meeting, to which we readily agreed but later wondered about the wisdom of that decision seeing that one of them was at least partially drunk. It was a new experience to have two heavily armed soldiers – one more senior than the other - stand in the aisle right in front of the raised platform in a relatively small grass-roofed 'church' building. They remained standing. To my hurried question to George 'What do we do now?' the instantaneous reply was 'Preach the gospel and preach it well, these men need to be saved'. I began to see soldiers in a new light. Another lesson. As the preaching proceeded the older man became somewhat agitated as the gospel message was evidently making him uncomfortable. It was another case of explaining sin, righteousness, and judgment to come. It wasn't too long before he chose to leave after speaking to the younger man. The young man was evidently ordered to remain, which he did until the end. A kind of armed captive audience but at least they both heard the gospel and maybe for the first time.

Lesson 2
Moscow

You can tell that the entire first visit to Angola made lasting impressions, just as a visit to central Africa does for many people. Our return journey to UK was also with Aeroflot on 23rd August through Budapest and Moscow back to London and Belfast, but without the reassuring company of Ruth Hadley. Luanda to Budapest was uneventful as was Budapest to Moscow. We were simply stopping a few hours in transit in Moscow airport.

As we queued to board the plane in Moscow, to our amazement a large contingent of people all dressed alike were ceremoniously allowed to bypass the rest of us and board the plane. Evidently they had some kind of priority, which seemed fair enough. Later we learned that they were members of an orchestra on their way to London to perform. Our progress plane-ward was quickly stopped when very officious men boarded the plane and started ordering off the plane some who were already seated, in order to make room for these important passengers. It became heated and unpleasant. All those ordered off were coloured – blatant discrimination. One such elderly lady who didn't seem to understand Russian was separated from her younger friend, probably her daughter, daughter-in-law, or some relative, and quite ruthlessly threatened with a gun to make her leave. We watched with increasing concern. The plane was now full though many were still waiting to board as well as us.

We were ordered to wait for the next flight and helpfully told that we could travel on it 'tomorrow', so that was a relief. Our baggage had gone on to London. Meanwhile we were to be lodged and fed in a nearby 'hotel' on the edge of the airport. The bedroom door had no lock, but we jammed something against it and tried to sleep. Food was provided. We were allowed into the dining area and the door was dutifully locked behind us – just as a precaution.

It only took a quick glance at the flight departures board to see that there were no London flights that day and no information beyond that. The airport foyer had no desks representing a variety of airlines. There was only an unmanned Aeroflot desk. That was it. What about a London flight the following day? Another night and the same exciting food. The cold beetroot soup was just about edible. The bread was supposed to be 'reconstituted' but we wondered what on earth it had been in its previous life. Maybe better not to know.

As we returned anxiously the following day to inspect the flight schedule it became obvious that there was still no

London flight. As we looked around we began talking with other equally frustrated passengers 'in the same boat', so to speak, waiting to catch the elusive London flight. We became aware of a couple with a young baby. Their hold luggage, like ours, was despatched on the plane and likely already in London. They needed nappies and baby milk but only had what was in their hand luggage. There was no way any of us could leave the airport and go into Moscow without a Visa which none of us had. We were all caught. It certainly sharpened our prayer life.

Among our group of abandoned travellers, we discovered that the husband of the couple with the baby had traveled previously through Moscow with school groups and spoke Russian. I found it interesting that a UK teacher would take groups of school children to Russia in those days of rampant communism. Anyhow he had a plan. He already knew or had discovered where the main Aeroflot office was located on the first floor up a staircase but with armed guards at the bottom and top of the staircase. As we gathered around and after much despairing discussion, he suggested to us that we all surrender our precious passports to him and to me – not quite sure why the rest trusted me! We would get past the armed guards, take the passports to the chief Aeroflot official upstairs and try to cajole or persuade someone that travel arrangements must be made for us all to anywhere in western Europe the following day if there was no flight to London. We all agreed as no other plan, never mind a better plan, was available. We had no way of finding out when the next flight to London might be – it might even be the next week.

Amazingly, complete strangers duly handed over their passports to him and to me. I looked at him and naively asked 'How do we get past the armed guards and over the two metal barriers?' His reply was simple. We were to jump the barriers, ignore the guards and the probability was they wouldn't shoot- if we moved fast enough. Probably. How I wished I had been a better hurdler in school sports, but it was too late. Margaret – and I suspect a few others – prayed as probably never before. We ran as quietly and as fast as we knew how, somehow got over the barriers and pushed our way past guards and reached the top of the stairs before the armed guards started shouting. Too late. We sprinted to the door of the office and walked in, passports in hand.

I was speechless as well as breathless. My friend did all the talking in what seemed to me fluent Russian and asked to speak with someone with the authority to make the desired bookings. He met with a blank wall as the first person walked off for lunch after demanding that we leave but nobody actually looked keen to physically throw us out. A second person was little better until my companion firmly grabbed a nearby phone on the desk and a telephone book. As he explained to me later, he demanded action, otherwise he would start phoning – I never did ask exactly who he would phone. Other airlines? Whatever. There was a thaw and a reluctant willingness to help.

It was now my job to try to keep family groups together as bookings were made to Helsinki, Brussels, Berlin, Rome, Paris – anywhere outside of Russia. As the bookings proceeded nicely we decided that he, his wife and baby, and Margaret and I must remain to the last after ensuring that everyone else got away first. For Margaret and me I opted for Paris as I spoke some fairly rusty French- well maybe quite rusty.

I was further amazed that he also managed to cajole the helpful official to make onward bookings for everyone right back to London, the original destination, and was willing to provide the needed paperwork. It really was quite helpful. We were grateful.

Can you imagine the delight as we re-joined the group impatiently waiting downstairs? The guards no longer took any notice of us, thankfully, and allowed us to pass without any need to show off our recently acquired hurdling skills. Can you imagine?

What a joy to leave Moscow and arrive in civilised Paris. We gladly presented the 'onward' booking papers so kindly provided in Moscow but were asked where we received them. When we replied, we were told that they were worthless but in line with some Geneva convention they would be honoured though British Airways would never be refunded by Aeroflot. To be honest we didn't much care as long as we got to London. At that stage we would almost have volunteered to swim the channel. Well, almost.

It was quite amazing that in all the apparent multi-national confusion of Heathrow, there in a storage area for unclaimed baggage were our suitcases safely waiting for us and intact, untampered with. What a relief. We had wondered would we ever see them again. We very happily bought our tickets back to Belfast. The joys of travel.

Above and beyond it all the Lord had allowed us to be left behind in Moscow but provided us with an English fellow-traveller who spoke fluent Russian. How could anyone arrange that?

Chapter 3
IRELAND AGAIN

Lesson 1
Back to teaching in Ballymena.

Teachers will know only too well the feelings of returning to an apparently more humdrum life after an exciting holiday in some exotic place, but our feelings went beyond that. Moscow was a little too exciting for our taste with irrational fears of ending up forgotten in some unpronounceable gulag. Both of us had enjoyed our teaching, the profession into which the Lord had guided us and in which we had much satisfaction beyond the usual frustrations of any job.

Margaret had been teaching Chemistry and Biology, first in Magherafelt Technical College and then was very happy when she was offered a job in Cambridge House Girls School in Ballymena. I had started off in Cullybackey Secondary School, followed by becoming the Head of the English Department in Dunclug Secondary School before having ten great years in Ballymena Technical College with about half my timetable 'A' level English Language and Literature. Life was good as were the salaries.

As the year after our visit to Angola progressed, both of us became more unsettled as we realised that anyone with our qualifications could happily do our teaching jobs but not everyone could fill the much-needed roles that we felt the Lord was calling us to in Angola.

We agonised as we wrestled with the increasing conviction of what we should do. It would be much more comfortable and certainly financially less risky just to stay in our jobs, keep on in our deep involvement in our local assembly where I had been asked to be an elder alongside an excellent group of highly motivated godly men.

As to 'living by faith' with no guaranteed income, now that was a scary idea if not even a bit foolish. We were unknown among Brethren assemblies and with our background of what were considered innovations in our assembly, clearly we would not be flavour of any month or year. None of the surrounding local assemblies would be likely to take any interest or support us either prayerfully or financially. Sure enough, as it turned out, most didn't but the Lord touched the hearts of individuals in what we thought of as some surprising places. As the Lord's servants we never lacked what we needed. The Lord saw to that.

It was made worse by the fact that Dunclug Gospel Hall, though doctrinally extremely orthodox, did not conform perfectly to all the accepted stricter norms of many mid-Antrim local Brethren assemblies. Initially we had no musical instrument, but later introduced a piano. With very good numbers of young people attending our youth meetings, we started Every Boys Rally and Every Girls Rally, in which both leaders and young people wore uniforms. The lives of many young people were being touched. They were hearing the gospel in an informal setting and quite a number professed faith in Christ. The annual summer Camps for young people of secondary school age were equally unacceptable to some. Yes, they were innovations, but were a wonderful opportunity to see the Lord bring many to faith in Christ.

Because of what was euphemistically called 'the Troubles' in Northern Ireland, it seemed wiser to hold the summer Camps in Scotland. That's where Nat Rodger's Scottish roots were a real blessing. He had contacts and invaluable local information. He and Jenny were the heart and soul of the Camp work. If I recall correctly, Liz Beattie and her cousin cooked at the first camp but then a certain young man seemed to like more than just Liz's cooking. She married Girvan and became Liz MacCorkell.

Margaret and I would regularly take our car and precede by a few days the main party of campers and take with us the two cooks, the two Jennifers – Jennifer Hamilton and Jennifer Kerr. Both were well qualified and very capable. It was truly a pleasure to work with such committed gifted colleagues. Camp meals were excellent; there never were any justified complaints.

In theory Margaret and I led those Camps but the reality was that we had such totally committed reliable young people around us as leaders with varying responsibilities that our task was made really simple.

Numbers grew. We shall never forget standing at an upstairs window in a school we had hired watching as two fifty-seater buses drove up to the entrance. We concluded that we must be quite mad. The Lord was very gracious as at one Camp twelve young people professed faith in Christ and as far as we know, have gone on with the Lord. Among other excellent speakers – like Alex Farrell, George Hall and Alex Courtney, Reggie Fry stood out and the Lord used him with his selection of colour coded 'letters' to lead many to Christ. His goal was to speak personally privately to every camper, and he made a determined effort to do so.

Not only were we greatly blessed in those camps by having an excellent team of very capable reliable young people who took their allocated leader responsibilities seriously but among the leaders were some with musical skills whether piano or guitar.

Camps continued from 1973 in New Prestwick Baptist Church Hall until 1984 in Dunseverick Primary School. Other speakers included Ed Jaminson and Willie Walker. When you put so many lively young people together, clearly we had lots of fun and an end of Camp party that may have raised some eyebrows.

One memorable phrase sticks in the memory. Isn't it amazing how we forget important things but easily recall what would be much better forgotten? The whole group was divided into teams for ease of organization under their allocated leader with an appropriate name. Stephen Hamill was just such a leader, and he came up with the name for his team – Hamill's Haemorrhoids. Mercifully none of the campers had any idea as to what a haemorrhoid might be as they happily rhymed 'I'm a Hamill's Haemorrhoid'. We inwardly vainly hoped that they might not relate such details to their parents back at home.

Lesson 2:
Could God want us to leave teaching and go to serve Him in Angola?

Having visited Angola despite the civil war, it did make an impression that not even normal teaching and the conveniences of Ballymena life could erase. The civil war sounded terrible from abroad, but Angola is a huge country the size of the land area of the UK, France, Spain and part of Portugal. War could be raging in one of its eighteen provinces while in most of the rest of the country life continued with relatively little danger. There would always be a risk that it could spread, and the key would be in assessing how quickly.

The Lord was speaking to us both through His Word and through interested close friends who were praying for us and keeping up to date with our thinking. It was almost like concentric circles. Personal conviction before the Lord, a few trusted friends who knew us well and then at a later stage we would have to consult the whole group of elders of our local assembly. Eventually we plucked up courage to ask to speak with the elders as a group. To our utter amazement one of them said 'We were wondering what was keeping you so long'. They already perceived and had prayerfully concluded that it was the Lord's will for us to serve Him in Angola or wherever the Lord might lead us and were willing to commend us to the grace of God. For quite some time, they had been waiting for us to speak with them. We found that a reassuring lesson.

One other experience merits mentioning. On the last occasion that I was asked to preach the gospel in Dunclug Gospel Hall before we were due to leave for language-learning in Portugal, I was concerned that I hadn't seen anyone come to Christ recently. I preached my heart out. I had quietly secretly asked the Lord to confirm our thinking by saving a soul that night. I was disappointed when no one professed to be saved that evening. Can you then imagine my delight when the following day a young man came to our house to tell us that he had trusted Christ as His Saviour the previous evening in his own home. How gracious is the Lord in dealing with our lack of faith?

Chapter 4
PORTUGAL
LANGUAGE-LEARNING AND MORE

So, after much heart-searching and with many misgivings we decided that we would resign from our teaching posts at the end of the 1982/83 school year and head to Portugal to learn Portuguese in Lisbon. It was amazingly scary arriving at the end of the month without the predictable pay cheques. How on earth would we survive with no teachers' pay? Had God not been teaching lessons about trusting Him before? That was fine in theory.

With some trepidation we had decided that we would live 'by faith', meaning totally depending on the Lord to meet our financial needs. So, we had no guaranteed income from any source but would accept gratefully what believers would send us guided by the Holy Spirit. We would never ever ask anyone for money, nor would we write so-called Prayer Letters with thinly veiled requests for money masquerading as 'making the need known'. We would make our needs known to the Lord alone and trust Him.

Lesson 1
Lisbon

We had already got to know Alf and Clella Poland, a lovely missionary couple who had lived in Lisbon for many years. Alf was Irish, southern Irish, with an Irish sense of humour, a mischievous streak and an excellent supply of Irish jokes –

what else? It is my considered opinion that no one without a healthy sense of humour should ever even consider becoming a missionary, though I can't support that idea with a Bible verse.

Clella was Canadian and reliably highly organized. They spear-headed an excellent radio gospel programme 'Dois dedos de conversa'- literally 'two fingers of conversation'; a chat. It was a superb radio technique of a short daily programme of general interest leading into a concise gospel message and all spoken by a male Portuguese believer with an endearingly resonant broadcasting voice.

The Polands welcomed us wholeheartedly and not only offered us accommodation but helped organize privately a retired Portuguese teacher who was a believer. She had lived and taught in Angola and her father had helped compile an academically highly respected Portuguese dictionary. One unforeseen benefit of her teaching was not only that she prayed with us, but she also taught us how to pray in Portuguese. Praying demands a special form of the verb which she helpfully explained as used mainly for one's wife/husband, a child, the dog, and God. Who would ever have thought of such a thing? She also helped us to retell Bible stories. What a blessing was Dona Elisama, a kindly elderly lady with a passion for her own language. As winter arrived it was wonderful to sit at her small round table with a heavy tablecloth that almost touched the floor, but underneath was a special pan filled with charcoal giving out a comforting steady heat. I never understood why we weren't all poisoned by carbon-monoxide. At least we had warm feet and legs. There was no central heating.

Later, thinking that it would be good for us, the Polands helped us rent a room in the home of a Portuguese lady who lived in Amadora. She spoke no English. It nearly drove both her and us completely crazy. She had a beautifully crafted grand-father clock right outside our bedroom door. The woodwork was absolutely lovely. It chimed every fifteen minutes throughout the night giving us the full Westminster treatment on the hour every hour. On one occasion when she went out, I foolishly ventured to twiddle a lever hoping to silence the beast. Instead, I merely altered it to a different chime which of course I didn't realise until it functioned perfectly after she had returned. My ingenuity apparently was not appreciated. No idea why.

How do you make a phone call when you can't yet be understood face to face? Again with Clella Poland's untiring assistance, we rented a flat in Costa de Caparica just outside of Lisbon and were enrolled at Lisbon University for a structured beginner's course. It included the use of a language lab which Margaret didn't appreciate but I enjoyed. Learning Portuguese was a long struggle, not made any easier by the fact that we were not teenagers. Margaret with her scientific background wanted to wait until every phrase was precisely accurate. I bumbled away happily, sometimes right and more often wrong, but more or less comprehensible with a dose of patient intelligent guesswork.

Balmy Lisbon autumn evenings were permeated by the unmistakable unforgettable whiff of chestnuts being roasted over charcoal, served up in a poke of newspaper. Unforgettable for a different reason were the hot afternoons spent rhyming off lists of very forgettable nouns and verbs under the shade of distinctive-smelling pine trees. The final insult was to be told by a whippersnapper son of a Christian couple that we were very stupid. We had made some stumbling attempt at polite conversation. Language learning is wonderful for your teacher's confidence, to say nothing of whatever little pride or self-esteem you might have left, but you must smile.

We had taken our car with us to Portugal only to learn that at that stage of the UK joining the European Union, it could only remain for six months without paying hefty import taxes. There was no alternative but to make an unforeseen trip back to N. Ireland about Christmas time. Driving to Portugal in summer was lovely but the Pyrenees in winter with snowfalls was another matter. We booked both ourselves and our car on a train to Paris.

We were in a compartment with an elderly Portuguese lady travelling to visit her family in Paris. As we attempted to practise our recently acquired language skills, we were quickly convinced we still had much to learn as the lady told us that at the border the train would have its wheels changed. Who ever heard of such a thing as changing wheels on a train? A puncture on a train? There must be some mistake. Sure enough, at the French border, the doors were all locked, the train was jacked up carriage by carriage, one bogy removed and replaced by another with a different gauge. She smiled knowingly and we knew our disbelief had shown.

But the restaurant car was also removed. We had counted on buying food on the train as indicated on the brochure. The dear lady realised we were unprepared and very generously shared the copious delicacies she had brought with her, and they were very good. How wonderful is the Lord in guiding His children to the right carriage where they would be well fed and watered? He didn't even need ravens. Another lesson?

We bought a different car and returned to Portugal. After spending some time in Lisbon and making at least some progress in Portuguese, we realised that the academic learning bit was passed and that what we needed was lots of conversation. However, life in a capital city tends to be fast and furious with little time for stilted conversation with semi-incoherent foreigners. After meetings with fellow believers both we and they had to dash to catch a tram, bus, or train which tend not to wait for stragglers. Many times we risked life and limb sprinting, well - running as fast as we could -

down narrow cobble-stone Lisbon streets some of which had been dug up by a utilities company. We dared to cross narrow muddy planks at full speed. Otherwise, we would have had to wait another hour to catch the last bus.

Lesson 2
Serious news from Angola

While we were still language learning in Lisbon there was a serious development in Angola. One evening on BBC World Service Radio we heard that UNITA (União Nacional para a Independência Total de Angola – the National Union for the Total Independence of Angola) had captured five westerners at Cazombo. We hastily counted the missionaries whom we knew would be likely to be there, Emily Rowntree, Eva Warke, and Patricia Steen, all from Northern Ireland, and two Canadian nurses, Marion Wilson and Norah Draper. There was a hurried search for a telephone box - before the advent of mobile phones- in Costa de Caparica and a call to Alf Poland. He hadn't heard the news but listened to the next broadcast. With considerable difficulty, he contacted a UNITA representative in Lisbon and the news was confirmed. He alerted Echoes of Service in England who in turn made contact with MSC (Missionary Service Committee) in Canada, their sister organization.

As it turned out, with sublime confidence UNITA had announced their great coup before it actually took place. They kidnapped only two lady missionaries. Patricia Steen had not been well, so Emily Rowntree and Eva Warke drove her across the border to get medical help at Chitokoloki Hospital in Zambia. That left only the two Canadian nurses. They were taken and forced to walk, mostly at night, the long journey of about 1,000 klms (625 miles) through mosquito-infested swamps, rivers and 'bush' in the wet season the whole way to Jamba where UNITA had their headquarters. The world's media was summoned to Jamba just before Christmas to show off the captives, proving to the world that UNITA controlled all that country which the government claimed to control but hadn't succeeded in locating this large contingent of UNITA soldiers with their captives. It was considered by UNITA a marvellous PR opportunity that attracted the western world's assembled news media. Afterward, the two nurses were released in time for Christmas.

The Canadian nurses told their story revealing the extreme hardships endured but also their deep respect for the consideration of the UNITA troops detailed to escort them. The soldiers were evidently given very stern instructions on how to treat the ladies. No soldier physically touched them unless when they were asked to do so to help them over very difficult terrain. Afterwards they expressed their admiration for the thoroughness of all aspects of organization in Jamba, including their medical facilities but both were traumatized by their experience. These events changed everything for us.

Lesson 3
Espinho

So, with no let-up in the Angolan civil war, we deemed it wise to remain in Portugal but advantageous to move up north to hopefully a less hectic pace of life where we might find those willing to talk without receiving much of a reply. It worked. We went to live in a semi-underground apartment beneath the rented property of a commended full-time couple, the husband Portuguese with the reputation of being a good language teacher, his wife an English lady. Viriato and Ruth Sobral. They were most kind and supportive. Sadly, with little natural light, the apartment was very cold in winter without central heating or a fireplace. A 'Superser' gas heater we bought gave out not only lovely heat but lots of moisture. Walls ran with condensation.

Margaret began having frequent throat infections that would respond only temporarily to antibiotics. She had to stay at home while I attended lots of meetings where I began speaking more frequently in stilted Portuguese. None of these rural halls had any form of heating despite the cold and the damp. We had little choice but to return to N. Ireland for medical help for Margaret. Sadly, her tonsils were being infected every winter even after several return trips to Northern Ireland.

One peculiarity of our stay in Espinho brought us another lesson. Despite our weakness in the language, we slowly noticed that there was a distinct slant on all the teaching we were listening to. Over time we also discovered that there were assemblies other than those which we were 'allowed' to attend. Unwittingly we were classified by association with one side in a historical theological argument that had arisen out of the desire to avoid the extremes of charismatic teaching. I quickly had to do some homework and all in Portuguese on the whole charismatic discussion, speaking in tongues, etc. an issue that had not been in contention in the assemblies with which we had historically been associated. It slowly dawned on us that, by association, we were seen as being on the side of an argument with which in reality we could not heartily agree. We were not charismatics and did not agree with unbiblical so-called 'speaking in tongues', but neither did we agree with the unbalanced arguments being sincerely taught on the other side. It reinforced the lesson that for new workers, it is vital to know the theology of preceding workers and the work already in existence in order to ensure future happy working conditions. Otherwise, much sorrow and sadness can result when fellow workers cannot labour together harmoniously for doctrinal or indeed any reasons. New missionaries need to be sure that they are truly welcomed and are in sufficient harmony doctrinally with their proposed future colleagues. It was a hard lesson.

Lesson 4
Penafiel

We decided before the Lord to move away and go to another area, much further north, where there was real need and only a very weak existing small assembly that was going through a traumatic experience because of the marriage breakdown of their Portuguese leading worker. In some respect, it was out of the frying pan and into the fire. We eventually managed to rent a comfortable apartment in Penafiel after several refusals once it was discovered that we were not Roman Catholics. We paid over the odds to a R.C. couple who valued money above their avowed religion.

To our surprise, it was in North Portugal, in Penafiel, that we first met with witchcraft. We were quite expecting to meet it in Angola but not in what seemed to us like a European civilised country. How wrong we were.

One morning when we opened the front door of our apartment, we saw a small flowering branch laid quite deliberately right across our doorstep. We had heard from our Christian friends of such things happening to others but never imagined it might happen to us. They had also informed us that this was a sign that the people in that house were being cursed and bewitched by those who claimed to have special evil powers that could even cause death. Aware that some neighbours were watching closely, I lifted the branch and very deliberately broke it into small pieces and threw it into a rubbish bin. We simply asked the Lord for

His continuing protection and if possible, an opportunity to witness to whoever was responsible. We never did discover who it was but it highlighted if it needed highlighting, that we were in a spiritual battle for the minds and souls of people held in the fear and ruthless spiritual slavery of Satan.

Even more amazing was what our Christian friends went on to tell us. They were aware that many blocks of apartments had their own known resident witch whom the residents would consult on a whole range of issues and at the same time they would attend Mass on Sunday. The more we discovered the more shocking it became as we learned of the intertwining of witchcraft and Roman Catholicism.

It was also in Portugal that Margaret was confronted with a demon-possessed woman. It was in a lady's Bible study and prayer time. She had been warned that a disruptive woman might attend as she had done on some previous occasions. Sure enough, when Margaret began to mention the Cross of Christ, this woman became exceedingly agitated, shouting and making strange sounds. Likewise, when the ladies decided to pray, that same reaction was provoked by any mention of the blood of Christ. Such a violent reaction was clear evidence that there was a spiritual battle going on in the life of that woman who had permitted Satan to take control of her mind and thinking. Equally clearly, she desperately needed God's salvation and the power of the Holy Spirit to dispel forever satanically controlled spirit forces. That can only happen alongside true repentance and determined abandonment of all that is in sinful rebellion against God.

Summer weather was great but come winter, some meetings were held in a bare unfinished house basement with no windows at all. We persisted, making full use of Marks & Spencer's best thermal underwear in multiple layers until we looked rather like a Michelin man that would not be hurt even if he fell over. Can you have a Michelin woman?

Predictably Margaret's throat infections returned. Equally predictably eventually after no adequate local medical help was available, we were obliged to return to Northern Ireland for medical attention for Margaret.

Sadly, on various occasions, when we mentioned that we had been living in Portugal, medical professionals back in Northern Ireland, simply insisted that she would be fine once we returned to the lovely warmth and heat of Portugal. Looking back, they can be excused as it would seem that they were influenced by their memories of hot Algarve summer holidays without realising that the north of Portugal winter climate was much like the UK but in those days most buildings were without cavity walls or a dampproof layer and certainly very few had central heating. Eventually, one surgeon said he really didn't want to remove her tonsils but on our insistence that he should go ahead, he reluctantly complied. Her throat infections never returned. We decided nonetheless it was essential to move further south to a more temperate climate away from the extreme winter rigours of the northern mountainous region. It was obvious that we couldn't cope with the intense cold in unheated houses and halls.

Lesson 5
Caldas Da Rainha

So, we moved to Caldas da Rainha where we were able to rent a flat on the first floor above a restaurant.

While living there, a visit back to see Alf and Clella Poland in Lisbon was always welcome, so when I was invited to share in a weekend conference in Lisbon we packed our things and went. As it was between the seasons we packed both lighter summer clothes and heavier winter ones to be sure we were ready for all eventualities.

An added bonus was that we had heard of the opening of the first big supermarket or hypermarket in Lisbon. Before that, there was only an abundance of smaller shops of every hue. It couldn't be missed, so we deviated a little and enjoyed seeing a much wider range of goods and many at really tempting prices, so we did it justice. On returning to our minibus, we discovered the doors all unlocked and all our goods gone – clothes – winter and summer, keyboard, briefcase with my Bible and lots of teaching notes, books – everything. We had taken into the hypermarket the money we were prepared to spend but left all our belongings safely locked in our vehicle. We didn't even have enough money left to pay the rather expensive motorway toll on our route home. We were obliged to borrow some money from a missionary colleague in Lisbon to get us home.

When we settled our heads back home in Caldas we realised that money could replace all that we had lost but how could I replace that much prized Bible with its handwritten additional notes, the fruit of listening to many Bible teachers in addition to my own regular study?

I recall somewhat sullenly questioning as to how or why God could allow this to happen when I needed my Bible to take with me to Angola. Days passed. We received a telephone call from a Portuguese-speaking lady who inquired as to whom she was speaking. Our surname is neither easily pronounced by English speakers or Portuguese speakers nor all that easily spelled out over the phone. She explained why she had telephoned.

This lady was returning home from shopping and had found some books lying beside the kerb and some others underneath a parked car. She gathered them up, took what she could carry home, and hid the rest where she could return later and retrieve them. Inside one book she found a label with a name, address and telephone number so she was trying the phone number. She guessed that this one book must be of some value to the owner as it had additional handwriting in the margins and between lines. I nearly shouted HALLELUJAH down the phone but wisely restrained myself.

She was rather nervous about meeting up with us foreigners, so settled on meeting at a certain Police Station. We agreed on the day and time. Later she changed her mind and invited us to her home. A single lady looking after an elderly mother. She had no idea what a Bible was and never had owned one. We had carried a Portuguese Bible with us and over a cuppa marked some passages that we read together from her newly acquired Bible. We tried to explain as simply as possible the marvellously good news of salvation. It was a pleasant journey back home with a reclaimed Bible. Did the Lord have a hand in the whole sequence of events? Did a lady and her mother need to hear the gospel simply explained? Did the Lord hear my sullen complaint about losing my precious Bible?

In Portugal, one of the highlights of each summer was that the Lord graciously gave us the opportunity to participate in one of our earlier enthusiasms – camps for young people. They had been such a blessing in Dunclug. So it was that we took a carload of believers to assist in the manual work of helping to prepare a campsite at a most delightful secluded rural spot in the mountains. The Director of the camp at Palhal, a Senhor Fontura, a very gifted capable preacher and teacher made us very welcome. He had been illiterate when he was saved but learned to read and write and became an avid reader and a dedicated Bible student. In time he became an enthralling speaker with such an oratorical fluency and command of his language that we often listened fascinated to his teaching of the Scriptures and his passionate preaching of the gospel. To this day I recall a moving heartfelt gospel message he gave on Judas Iscariot.

He was also a gracious man willing to listen to a suggestion from a much younger man introducing a new concept. I had taken with us to Portugal a 35mm projector and a selection of Moody Bible Institute 'Fact and Faith' films. They had been useful in evangelism in N. Ireland presenting the gospel in a novel but challenging way. If I recall correctly, Theo Hewitt (Norway) and Dr.Donald Gaston used them in an Orange Hall in Cullybackey and effective they were. We also used them in the Oasis young people's outreach work on Broughshane Street in Ballymena.

When I first suggested the possibility of using them at the Palhal Camp for teenagers, not unreasonably he expressed considerable hesitation but consented to allow us to show one film as an experiment. Quite rightly, Senhor Fontura was aware that not everything from the USA is desirable in evangelism. We chose 'The City of the Bees' projected onto a very large taut bed sheet suspended between two trees.

It was an outstanding success so that every evening of that week as darkness descended and the cicadas sang we had another Moody 'Fact and Faith' film as we sat comfortably in the summer evening warmth. Good conversations followed and young people were moved as the Holy Spirit challenged them. It was thrilling to see young people come to faith in Christ at Camps in Palhal.

That dear brother also invited me to give a short Bible Study each morning. That stretched my fluency in Portuguese as he kindly helped me to expand my vocabulary and corrected my inappropriate or ungrammatical expressions, but he did it in such an inoffensive way that highlighted his godly love of 'nothing but the best' in the Lord's work. He had been there himself. A valuable lesson.

Our time in Caldas da Rainha was filled with the challenge of trying to assist a Portuguese full-time couple Vitor and

Isobel Tavares who lived in Lourinhã and had the nearly impossible task of trying to assist several small struggling local churches in quite scattered locations. These included Caldas da Rainha itself but also Torres Vedras, Peniche, Lourinhã and Monte Redondo. That was an exceedingly heavy burden for them to undertake and with a young family of two girls. Not only that but distances were considerable, and the roads then were not like today. Many roads were of hard-wearing cobblestones but when only a few were missing they formed very sharp-edged holes that were lethal on tyres and the steering joints of vehicles to say nothing of jolting the nerves of the drivers.

Several of those little groups of believers were profoundly dispirited. As we tried to learn a little of the history of each group, we were also learning some hard lessons. First was the spiritual grip of Roman Catholicism that was so ingrained in every aspect of cultural, spiritual, and national life. It was traditionally intrinsically embedded in what it meant to be Portuguese. The Reformation had bypassed Portugal. Many had little or no knowledge whatsoever of the Scriptures before they came to know Christ Attending Mass was everything. Second came the weakness flowing from a lack of consistent systematic Bible teaching and trained gifted Bible teachers. That situation was not helped by unnecessary squabbles and divisions probably largely prompted more by pride and personality clashes rather than any profound doctrinal issues. We learned that past grievances were very hard either to forgive or forget.

That resulted in a distinct shortage of young people. Vitor and Isobel did a marvellous job of teaching and training what young people were left by bringing them together for special weekends of teaching, singing, lovely food, and good fellowship. Young people brought their friends. We had some little input in that work as well as we saw the strategic value of working with young people so that they would become keen committed followers of Christ using their God-given gifts and abilities. Sadly, some of the fellowships had no young people left.

So, we had no shortage of opportunities to preach, teach and encourage each Sunday alongside the constant need to gather believers midweek in homes for Bible Study and prayer. In some homes, the believers invited unsaved family members and neighbours so that evangelistic Bible studies were needed. What a privilege it was to explain the Scriptures and the simplicity of the gospel in homes where people could ask questions in the informality of the home. The experience of leading evangelistic Bible studies in Dunclug had been a useful preparation.

It was a joy to see some profess faith in Christ and also to see some take the courageous step of being baptized by immersion as believers after listening to the clear teaching of Scripture regarding the need for believers to witness publicly to their newfound faith in Christ alone as their Saviour. It also indicated their total break with the RC faith in which they had been brought up. If needed, it reinforced our conviction regarding the value of clear Bible teaching both from a platform and the probably equal value of explaining the gospel around a kitchen table in homes. Probably the joy of sharing simple meals together contributed to breaking barriers and building trust.

Those were busy and tough years with lots of hard work and relatively little to show for it, apparently like most outreach in western European countries. Sadly, we were obliged to return to Ireland for a prolonged period of time in need of a time of rest and medical help when I was unwell. Margaret went back temporarily to teaching but in Cambridge House Boys School as boys were then being admitted alongside the girls to become a co-educational school. She hated it because of the indiscipline of the disinterested pupils but courageously persisted to keep us afloat financially.

Chapter 5
A VISIT TO ZAMBIA

As time passed the civil war in Angola seemed interminable with one side funded by excellent supplies of oil while the opposition was funded by diamonds and precious metals. Leaders grew wealthy while their people starved and to those who had the funds, buying arms was not a problem as arms dealers from many countries were keen to oblige. Russia was keen to support the communist government they had helped to install by making use of those 10,000 Cuban troops aided by their 1,000 Russian 'advisers'.

In our frustration, we decided that it might be time to investigate if we could reach Chokwe people and make a start on learning Chokwe in Northwest Zambia where tens of thousands of Angolans had fled for refuge from constant fighting, bloodshed, starvation and death. A huge orderly camp had been established at Maheba in Northwest Province.

So we contacted Mr Kenneth Barker and his wife, Doreen, missionary colleagues in Zambia, who did their utmost to help us at every turn. Mr Barker in Chingola even located a vehicle belonging to a missionary who had been obliged to return to his home country because of persistent illness. We wrote to that missionary in N America and a sale for an excellent pickup vehicle was agreed and we received the documents and one set of keys in the post in Ballymena. Mr Barker even arranged for it to be brought to where he lived in Chingola and serviced ready for use. How could such kindness ever be rewarded? It was obvious that we would be made very welcome at least by some of the missionaries to stay and work in Zambia.

Such helpfulness in supplying us with an excellent vehicle enabled us to freely visit many mission stations in Zambia, meet the missionaries and see their work. That was from 23rd April-22nd Sept 1987. We quickly discovered that the Chokwe refugees from Angola were widely scattered over a considerable area and entrance by foreigners to the massive camp for Angolan refugees at Maheba was closely controlled by the Zambian government, even just for a brief visit. Incidentally, as the picture shows, we quickly learned that as we travelled around there was almost always something needing to be transported from one place to another.

One visit was memorable for the wrong reason. We were made very welcome at Dipalata and enjoyed a pleasant evening walk near the river, not realising that it was a perfect place and time for mosquitoes. We stayed a few days and then proceeded towards Kalene Mission Station and hospital. It was a lengthy tiresome journey. The last part of the road was very rough so I was very tired but surprised by an exceedingly severe headache. Relief at arriving was tempered by a headache and a feeling that not all was due to tiredness. Malaria was diagnosed and the appropriate treatment prescribed. It was a good hospital with two experienced ex-pat medical missionary doctors. What a relief when I began to feel better but somehow it was taking longer than expected to recover some lost energy. To many, it may not make any sense, but I quickly discovered that for me the distinctive smell of bacon frying would produce the nausea that was an excellent indication of malaria. When I thought I had more or less recovered, a kind invitation to have a meal in the home of Jim Rennie, one of the doctors, revealed the unwanted truth. I deteriorated rather quickly and did not respond to any treatment so eventually because of my delirious sickness there was no choice but to put me on an IV drip. I faded in and out of hallucinations and semi-consciousness but after 6 days with a quinine drip I was not making progress, rather the opposite. That was the ultimate treatment. Normally when quinine doesn't work for malaria the patient needs to have made his last will and testament. Margaret was exhausted as she never slept, keeping careful vigil that the drip would not stop during the night or develop a fatal air bubble. I gather that precautionary preparations were made to ensure adequate wood would be available in the woodwork shop to take me to my final resting place.

On a Sunday evening the whole staff gathered for a time of urgent prayer asking the Lord to spare my life if it were His will. Quite unexpectedly the hospital pharmacist, Mary Stewart from England, began to think that a certain drug that was in very scarce supply might help. Her hasty search of the pharmacy produced a small supply. From the following day, I began to make slow but steady progress. A visit planned for only a few days to a missionary hospital – as we are not medically trained – stretched into a few weeks before I was able to contemplate driving again. Both very capable ex-pat doctors suggested that we might carefully consider returning to the UK and remaining there. That was not a welcome idea, but we decided to pray very definitely about that possibility.

Our foolishness was adequately displayed by my insistence that we must visit the renowned Victoria Falls as we would never ever set foot again in Zambia. That much we had quite definitely decided.

It was going to be a very long tiring journey, so we stayed with Ballymena friends, John Buick and his wife Janette who were then based in Kitwe so made an early start the next morning to cover just over 840 klms /500 miles that day from Kitwe to Livingstone and the Victoria Falls. I recall commenting to Margaret, or was it really complaining, various times 'these Falls had better be good'. It probably wasn't the best way to recuperate from a near-death illness.

In those days vehicle traffic was light, but Police roadblocks were very plentiful. I still recall an interesting session at one Police roadblock where the roadworthiness of our vehicle was questioned. I was asked to switch on side lights, headlights, full and dipped beam, flashing indicators, etc which were all OK until I was asked about my 'weepers'. I honestly had no idea what 'weepers' might be and had no choice but to request the policeman to repeat his request several times, indeed until he was getting quite cross at my stupidity. His attempt at actions helped me to realise that he was referring to the windscreen wipers. Of course, 'weepers' were wipers – everyone knew that.

The Victoria Falls exceeded our expectations and the few days spent there revived our travel weary bones before we made our way back to N. Ireland to reconsider prayerfully what the Lord was wanting us to learn and to do. It was a disconcerting and profoundly discouraging time.

Chapter 6
ANGOLA AT LAST

Not very long afterward, in 1991 the Lord intervened. We were invited by Marjorie Beckwith, a Canadian missionary, to go to Luanda to help with the teaching in a one-month Bible School in Viana on the outskirts of Luanda. We applied for and were granted a Visitor's Visa which would permit us to stay a few months. So, we booked our return tickets and went. While there, we evaluated that the security situation in Luanda had improved considerably as a Peace Accord had been signed, so the war was over. With only a Visitor's Visa, we tentatively wondered if we could somehow have it converted into a proper Residence Permit. As in most countries, the law was clear that it was obligatory to leave the country and re-apply from outside to obtain a Residence Permit. We made an application and quite extraordinarily and totally beyond our control, our Residence Permits were granted. Was the Lord saying something? We stayed on in Luanda with the hope that we would be able to move inland to Biula Mission Station once the war ended properly all over the country, as it must.

Lesson 1
The reality of Luanda

We knew Luanda would not be Lisbon. As an initial short-term provisional staging-post, we were made most welcome in the shared home of two very different missionary ladies.

One was a nurse who never married, Marjorie Beckwith, Canadian, who spoke fluent Chokwe having spent many years attending the sick in the small but very effective rural clinic at Biula, working alongside Ena Wiseman, also a nurse. The civil war had obliged her to move to Luanda, the capital, where she continued to encourage and help many Chokwe believers who also had fled to the capital for safety from all the ruthless confusion of the civil war. She was an incredibly patient caring lady who seemed just about unflappable but in reality, she was a deeply spiritual godly lady with a very generous heart – generous both with her time and her possessions, untiringly assisting her beloved Chokwes, some of whom seemed to take full benefit of her renowned generosity.

The other lady was Iris Floyd de Nascimento, an English lady, also a nurse, who spoke Luvale, having spent many years at Kavungu Mission Station in the remote eastern part of Moxico Province. She had married a Portuguese Angolan man but sadly later their marriage failed. They had rented a government-owned pleasant three-bedroomed 7th-floor apartment in Rua Commandante Gika in Luanda which remained hers even after her husband abandoned her. She was an excellent cook and very hospitable and loved to offer accommodation to visiting ex-patriot believers, providing lovely meals despite the scarcity of nearly everything. Under communist rule, there were no hotels where foreigners could stay as hotels were all government-owned and for the sole use of those to whom 'The Party' wished to offer accommodation. So, the Visitors Book was an amazing record of visiting believers from around the world. It included the signature of Franklin Graham, son of Billy Graham. We were told that there were times when some even slept – or attempted to sleep - on a mattress under the dining table. It was amazing how everyone was welcomed even at very short notice. That telephone line was a godsend link to the world even though you could spend hours waiting to get a connection to the outside world from the central telephone exchange. Those from abroad could at least telephone in – if they had sufficient patience.

When she was spending some time in England, Iris had given over her apartment to a missionary couple needing a place to stay, Charlie and Betty Shorten. They had been obliged to flee from the civil war in the south of the country. Amazingly when she returned, instead of re-possessing her apartment, she unselfishly decided to acquire from the communist government a plot of land (private property) being used as a rubbish dump. Then she also arranged to import from abroad a prefabricated four-bedroom bungalow in sections, made of metal sheeting that was erected on a steel structure that enabled the building to be up off the ground. It wasn't unheard of that the previous furry rubbish dump occupants scuttled around below. To acquire land and put a house on it was an amazing feat of patience, endurance, and utter determination. Yes, she was a determined but very capable lady with a truly big heart for all who loved the Lord whether Angolan or expat.

In reality, both Iris and Marjorie had big hearts for the needy and the Lord's people. Monthly they invited all the ex-patriot Christian missionaries they heard of to a Saturday afternoon in their home for a time of singing, prayer, fellowship, and an encouraging message from the Scriptures. Iris was exceedingly good at preparing lovely meals for everyone. That meeting was a lifeline for many in a very trying city. When they heard of a group of Filipino believers working in Luanda, they too were invited. Just being with believers in a normal home brought those Filipino Christians much joy. One played the guitar and how they loved to sing. Those were precious moments.

Among those who attended joyfully were several missionaries from Pentecostal churches, lovely believers. We prayed for each other and the various sometimes quite discouraging circumstances in a wide variety of local church fellowships. I recall after one brother in the Lord gave an excellent Bible talk, I suggested to him that I thought I really should join his church as he hinted strongly that it was wonderful to be able to speak in tongues. That ability I hastily agreed confirmed it for me. It was a serious attraction. I had struggled to learn Portuguese and was facing the possibility that we should both learn Chokwe so it would be so amazingly helpful to be able to do so without the hard slog of mastering complex grammar, learning lists of nouns, pronouns, verbs, and all the rest as it could take several years to be good enough to teach the Scriptures competently. I would be most grateful to the Holy Spirit for this mind-blowing shortcut.

I somewhat mischievously asked if that's how he spoke such good Portuguese, but he quickly clarified that he had to go to language school just like everybody else. So, I pressed the point that on the Day of Pentecost in Acts 2, even academically uneducated fishermen between them spoke fluently about a dozen different languages and spoke so proficiently that they were clearly understood by those who were native speakers. At that, he tried to convince me that 'his' speaking in tongues was different. He was unimpressed when, tongue in cheek, I commented that 'his' church could be held in contempt of the Trades Description Act in the UK for it clearly shouldn't have the word 'Pentecostal' in its name as it had nothing like an Acts 2 Pentecostal experience to offer. He seemed to get the message that I wouldn't be joining any church with such a deceptive name. That in no way undermines my earlier comment that he was a lovely godly brother in the Lord, and we continued to pray with and for each other in our monthly Saturday afternoon meetings.

That site for the temporary bungalow had another tremendous advantage. It was close to the airport and when necessary, was more or less within walking distance. Of course, it also enjoyed all the noise from the nearby airport and the prefabricated material from which it was constructed didn't include any soundproofing. The downside was that the airport was also partly military, so to the sounds of overloaded Antonov cargo flights were added the unmistakable screams of Russian MIG fighter jets. They had a habit of breaking the sound barrier at low altitude in celebration of a notable victorious hit on an enemy target. Not only could we read the markings on the planes, but we could also see clearly the pilots in their cockpits as they flew over the house at a dangerously low altitude.

The thin metal material wasn't exactly bullet-proof either. Being near the airport where lots of desirable goods were being stored offered an excellent target for thieves, one suspected sometimes with the help of 'insiders'. They were often chased by gun-toting police or army who had no shortage of ammunition, so bullets flew. One bullet pierced the thin roofing metal and embedded itself in the floor just short of the bed where a visitor had been sleeping the previous night. A bullet hole in a bedroom window was proof of an earlier hit. We needed bullet-proof curtains, but we never found the right shop.

On another occasion of police chasing suspected airport thieves, I found myself about to close the gate as bullets ricocheted off the wall and pillars. I was glad that I was then fairly slim as I aligned myself neatly with the pillar as the bullets whizzed off the other side. Such was life in Luanda. Never a dull moment.

What we thought and hoped would be only a short-term provisional staging post seemed unending and went on for more than a year. Even though the Shortens had retired back to North America if we were to stay long-term in Luanda that excellent apartment that we so badly needed was occupied temporarily. That was totally as had been agreed. She was a single lady missionary who likewise could not find alternative accommodation. Rents were horrendously expensive. You could pay up to £10,000 a month- yes per month - to rent a 3-bedroom terrace house with no garden and scarcely enough space to park a vehicle inside a high concrete wall and equally tall metal doors. Not many private people could afford those prices never mind evangelical missionaries.

The Angolan oil business was booming and nearly every international oil company had a foothold in Luanda. They had what seemed like endless money to pay astronomical rents. Remember Angola had been pumping almost as much oil as Nigeria. For years communist ideology prevented private building. Later with a sort of privatization, those close to the government and military 'obtained' private land and businesses. No foreigner or local person could legally start a business without an Angolan partner – a government or military official - who made no investment but had to be apportioned a substantial fraction of all profits just for the privilege. I don't know if that restriction is still in force.

For us, living with these two ladies was an unplanned experience. Our plan had been to move inland to Biula Mission Station where there were three houses and one had been allocated to us, the one where the Wisemans had lived. It was basically a soundly constructed house that could be made quite liveable. As the civil war ebbed and flowed, the opposition movement UNITA rapidly saw the blessing of a well-cared-for Mission Station with empty houses and a regular water supply. 'Our house' we learned had become the local UNITA opposition party HQ and not for the first time during the 30-year war.

So we attempted to readjust to doing something useful in Luanda. Very soon Margaret was encouraged to take charge of a Saturday morning children's Good News Club in the small back yard of the prefabricated house. There was no shortage of children in the nearby streets, and they came willingly. When at all possible, she liked to have a young local committed believer alongside her both to help and to learn as she accepted and coped with more and more responsibility.

Margaret also spoke at many ladies' meetings in nearby assemblies and usually had large numbers attending. On occasions, when it was deemed safe enough, she would take our Landrover with a full load of ladies. It was a time of fruitful ministry for Margaret. The ladies thoroughly appreciated her clear teaching of the Word. She never had an opportunity to teach 200 ladies in a ladies' meeting in Northern Ireland but that was a normal number in Luanda.

Likewise, she was asked to speak at ladies' conferences mostly in Luanda but there the attendance was larger. Her teaching was greatly appreciated. Looking back, she was glad that the Lord had over-ruled in allowing us to spend longer than we had originally planned in Portugal. We needed that extra time to gain fluency and confidence in teaching the Scriptures accurately. Slowly but surely we learned the lesson that the Lord's ways are always best even when we chafed and thought we knew better.

I tried to visit the various local assemblies and quickly discovered just how many there were and indeed how large some were with upwards of 300 members. While a Sunday visit to preach the gospel was an encouragement to them as some professed faith in Christ, it was obvious that there was a need for much more detailed regular Bible teaching but where and how should I begin?

Lesson 2
More small Bible Study groups

Past experience of leading small group Bible Studies was much more appealing. I was introduced by our missionary colleague Ruth Hadley to an existing series of inductive Bible Study books printed in Brazil called 'Seja um Obreiro Aprovado' (Be A Workman Approved). Many of the keener believers in Luanda had already studied Emmaus Bible Correspondence Courses – which incidentally are really excellent. The study of these Emmaus courses was sacrificially made possible by several totally dedicated Angolan very capable believers. I had already completed most of these Emmaus courses in English provided by Ed Jaminson who lived in Belfast. Ed was an ex-missionary to South American Spanish-speaking Bolivia. What transpired therefore was that I chose groups of ten men who had completed 20 Emmaus Courses. They were of different tribal origins, from different assemblies, and where an older man came, I insisted he had to bring a much younger capable man with him who was not from his family circle.

The reason was obvious. An assembly elder often wanted his son to be an elder even when his son was totally unqualified biblically or maybe not even a believer. Such was the tendency to want to establish a kind of family dynasty that could attempt to control a local assembly. Sadly, a not dissimilar desire to establish such a family dynasty or in some way favour the active participation of purely family members has also been seen outside of Africa.

Too often in African thinking, there is confusion between a village elder and a biblical assembly elder. As soon as a village elder professes faith in Christ, he is too often automatically regarded as an elder in an assembly. For many Africans, it would be unthinkable for him not to be recognized immediately as an elder in a local church.

In the 'Seja' groups we met once a week for two hours. Everyone would commit to completing homework which would be returned to me for marking with corrections and formed the basis of the start of the following lesson. That sounds easy but took a considerable amount of organization, time and commitment just to get all the homework collected and returned to me. Travel, like everything else in Luanda was time-consuming and difficult.

Word spread. These men were soon seen to be better equipped to preach and teach in their assemblies. Eventually, there were groups meeting almost every weekday. I would travel to those meeting in outlying assemblies as travel by minibus was difficult and expensive for these men, most of whom were internally displaced as refugees from war within their own country and unemployed. At its worst, it sometimes took two hours to drive to a study – and that was still inside Luanda - then two hours of study and another two hours to return home. 35^0 C with high humidity was not unusual in the rainy season.

Those Bible studies were immensely worthwhile. This was for me the highest priority – teaching the Scriptures daily to groups of ten motivated men who really were prepared to make considerable sacrifices to study and understand God's Word. One group met in our lounge. That method of study to me was profitable in that being informal anyone could ask questions at any juncture and any other questions that were troubling them. There was time both to ask questions and try to give guidance thoughtfully from Scripture. I also think it was good in that sometimes I simply was happy to say that I couldn't give an immediate answer because I honestly didn't know, but that I would go away, study the Scriptures and think about it prayerfully for the following week. I considered it essential not to pretend that I, the white missionary, had all the answers but to show them that I too needed to search the Scriptures before humbly suggesting tentative answers to some very difficult questions.

It also was useful to help them understand that on some matters, including teaching about future events, there must be room to differ respectfully and not to consider as an enemy someone who disagrees on some debatable prophetical matter regarding the future. It is not always easy to help others understand the difference between essential matters of faith and salvation and secondary matters over which even godly believers might hold a slightly differing view. I rapidly learned that too many believers wanted a very precise answer to which everyone must subscribe fully or risk being excommunicated and not allowed to remember the Lord in the Breaking of Bread. Without racial overtones, they wanted everything biblical to be totally clear-cut or 'black and white'.

It also gave time and opportunity to pray together. That was especially good for some of the younger men who would never dare to pray aloud in their home assembly. Some assemblies were quite large in number with tacitly accepted unwritten rules as to who could pray aloud and sometimes it was just the 'elders'. It was lovely to see how younger men prayed very tentatively at the start and then grew in confidence as they poured out their hearts in real meaningful prayer expecting the Lord to answer in accord with His sovereign will.

As we studied the Scriptures together with these men, we became more aware of the difference between the availability to us, English-speaking westerners, of additional helpful Bible study material and the relative paucity for them. Affordability was made all the starker in that the majority of them were internally displaced within their own country and found it nearly impossible to find employment. Some who had friends or relatives still in the diamond mining areas seemed to have unrevealed lines of financial support but that was a small minority. For most, funds were scarce as they struggled to manage the basics for living.

So, it was a joy when we discovered that Study Bibles in Portuguese were available from Brazil even though expensive when transport costs were taken into account. It was worth it however so that all of these men could have at least one Study Bible even if it meant we had to subsidise the price. We considered it an excellent investment for the future of God's kingdom.

As the years passed, men who were steadily growing in their understanding of the Scriptures continued to study with me once a week but were entrusted with the responsibility of leading their own group of ten men mostly from their own assembly taking them through the first years of the course. That way they progressed themselves and taught ten more. So the work was mushrooming with many groups meeting weekly to study the Scriptures and work out the practical implications in their lives, their marriages, their assemblies, and in practical outreach outside the walls of wherever they met.

The Holy Spirit seemed to really get a grip of the hearts of one group who met in Boa Vista. As we learned together how the Lord didn't just teach in the Temple or the synagogues but deliberately reached out and indeed commanded his disciples to 'Go' and not just to sit in their places of worship and say 'Come', they were challenged as to how and where they should 'go'. As they prayed about it, most of that group decided that they would accept a challenge that I had almost casually suggested. They were living quite near one of the large government prisons and knew at least a few people inside as well. So, they prayerfully set about obtaining all the clearances and permissions needed for a group of them to go once a month for one hour. Permission was granted. They went and preached the gospel inside the prison and started taking with them Emmaus Bible Correspondence Courses for those interested.

Imagine my surprise and shock when after some time 'my' Boa Vista students came back to me asking me to accompany them to prison. They made all the arrangements as by then the prison governor had got to know and trust them. My clearances were sought and granted. I was secretly wondering about the wisdom of me – a white man – going among thieves and murderers, some of whom openly confessed that they hated white men and would happily kill them. We also suspected that others were high on drugs and that some had severe mental problems that should have been receiving psychiatric treatment instead of imprisonment. The prison was grossly overcrowded.

The Sunday came. I met up with my friends who had prepared all permissions and they guided me in. The governor kindly welcomed me into his office, but the welcome quickly felt less welcoming when he explained that he had allocated four burly guards for my protection, one of whom would walk directly closely in front of me, another behind, and two more close by, one at each side. When I began to question the need, he firmly replied that it would be absolutely essential as we passed through the huge open yard jammed with prisoners, but once beyond the open yard, two would be enough. I couldn't really object. In prison, you do as you are ordered.

It was a sweaty walk through that open yard and not just because of the heat of the afternoon. Yes, I was afraid but quietly confident. It was an unusual experience walking virtually hidden behind a guard only a few centimetres in front of my nose, knowing that there was another equally close behind me.

I was amazed to find such a large congregation in the appointed room. And could they sing? There's nothing quite like a prison male voice praise choir. What a privilege. Can Africans sing? Will some Angolan prison male voice choir members form part of that choir in heaven that sings the praises of the Lamb? Their voices blended beautifully as they harmonised and of course, they couldn't sing so heartily standing still. They swayed and moved with superb coordination. Some told how they had come to faith in Christ while in prison. The skeptic in me wondered how many would still sing the Lord's praises and live a very different lifestyle when released. I preached the gospel to what was literally a captive audience and was amazed at how many wanted to talk personally afterward but sadly time was limited. Month by month that team of 'my' men continued faithfully preaching and teaching. Of course, they weren't 'my' men, they were the Lord's men doing the Lord's work with commitment, verve, and dedication, but I rejoiced in that the Lord had given me the inestimable privilege of being such a small part in their growing understanding of the wonder of the gospel of God's forgiveness and their desire to see others come to know their Lord – even prisoners convicted of murder. Did I hear echoes of Saul of Tarsus?

Those studies continued right up until we said our sad farewells. What cheered my heart was that as the years passed and the war situation eased in many areas with the arrival of relative peace, many of these men were beginning to visit the tribal areas from which they had fled. They were anxious to take the gospel back into their home districts. It was of the Lord that so many tribal groups were represented in those studies.

On one occasion as a group of men of the Songo tribe were preparing to take a trip back to their remote area, I asked if they had all they needed. I also foolishly asked if it would be

OK for me to go with them. They reluctantly explained what they expected. They would ride on the back of an open truck as far as the truck could go, then they would ride bicycles as far as the bicycles could go on bush paths. Eventually, they would have to leave the bicycles and walk the rest. I asked where they would sleep. In some areas they knew relatives or kind friends, in others where they knew no one, they were certain that a village headman would arrange somewhere for them to stay. They might even just sleep by the side of the path as they would feel secure in a group. They were itching to go and spread the gospel. One young man claimed to be one of the few known believers in his sub-tribe, so he was particularly enthusiastic.

Two things followed. They didn't have bicycles, so it was our pleasure to give them money to buy bicycles. Second, it became obvious that just as they said, there was no way an older man like me would survive such journeys. I must admit I eventually heartily agreed. These were young fit men used to such rigours and highly motivated to preach the gospel and teach the Scriptures to their tribal members, family members, and their friends. They would also do so with a much better understanding of all the cultural backgrounds of which I was totally ignorant. Reluctantly I had learned another lesson.

That was what made all the inconvenience well worthwhile. Men had studied the Scriptures and grasped the wonder of full free salvation by faith in Christ crucified that must result in a transformed lifestyle. Now they were counting it a privilege to take that same gospel to their own people in their own language. I spoke none of their tribal languages.

Everything else that I have written about pales into insignificance besides the joy of knowing that many of these men were keen to preach the gospel and teach God's divinely inspired Word guided and we trust empowered by the Holy Spirit. Only eternity will reveal the results.

Lesson 3
Life in Luanda

Luanda traffic was horrendously overcrowded, disorganized, and lawless. It was not for the faint-hearted. The unwritten rule was that if another vehicle only smashed your door or wing mirror, nobody stopped. I had strong wrap-round bull-bars fitted to the front of the Landrover to protect lights and bodywork. Now, of course, they are illegal in Britain but that was Angola. It became a kind of joke that frequently a large truck would pass so close that it straightened out the side part of the bull bars that then stuck straight out in front like a rhino horn. I made friends with a local capable welder who made a good living I suspect helped by my frequent repairs to the Landrover bull bars. He used to joke as I left, saying 'come back soon'.

The journey to Viana where the Camps were held and where we had a storage yard for containers passed through a very busy typical chaotically disorganised African market. People were only a metre or slightly more away, but sometimes even less from the sides of your vehicle. It was a nightmare driving through it very, very slowly. It was commonly accepted that very desperate people would deliberately throw themselves in front of a slow-moving vehicle driven by a 'wealthy' foreigner just to get the necessary 'compensation'- money, clothes, food - basically as much as they could extract from the guilty driver. The police were also on their side.

On one occasion the almost inevitable happened. I was driving slowly on the main road to Viana through that bustlingly overcrowded African-style market meaning that stalls and people were as close to the traffic as possible without actually blocking the road. A young girl was hit but not badly injured. We put her in the back and asked if there was anyone else with her. As normally happened an enraged crowd immediately gathered and started banging on the sides of the vehicle clearly mercilessly wanting to attack us and steal all in the vehicle. It was a very dangerous situation for all of us.

In the goodness of God, a policeman nearby saw the whole thing. He quickly jumped into the seat beside me and said 'Go' despite the milling crowd. When I hesitated, fearing I would injure or kill someone, he bellowed at me in Portuguese 'Just go'. With him clearly visible in the front, the crowd made way reluctantly and we fled the scene. Generous 'compensation' was paid after confirming that she was not seriously injured with only cuts and mild bruising. Wasn't it amazing again that the Lord had placed a sympathetic policeman so close to where a rural village girl would dash senselessly across a busy road? Not all policemen would have been so sympathetic. The girl came from a rural area where there were hardly any cars to worry about. She had just arrived recently in the maelstrom of Luanda traffic.

Luanda life, including driving, was always very stressful. Incidentally in those days, there was no such thing as car insurance, but you had to remember that most drivers carried a loaded pistol in the glove compartment and were not afraid to use it to settle any traffic accident disagreements. That was life.

Eventually after more than a year staying with our two dear missionary sisters, that seventh-floor flat was handed over to us and it almost seemed like the seventh heaven – at least for a while. Just to have our own space as a couple was wonderful. As time went on, we discovered that it had disadvantages as well. One drawback was that there was no way we could park our Landrover on the street overlooked by our flat. Security for vehicles was non-existent. It would be unlikely to be more than a few hours before a relatively new well maintained Landrover would be stolen – and possibly even by the police or a family member.

Just a few years earlier when Ruth Hadley was living in that same flat, a newish Landrover was stolen at gunpoint from a neighbour's yard. When she managed to get an interview with a high-ranking police officer, she spotted the Landrover parked within police premises. She was given an ultimatum in no uncertain manner. If she insisted on the return of her vehicle, her Visa would be rescinded immediately giving her 24 hours to leave the country permanently or she could simply leave quietly and never more mention who had evidently authorized the theft. She left. What can be done when high-ranking police officers are themselves the thieves or when their heavily armed underlings are obeying their orders?

That meant that we ended up continuing to park our vehicle in the security of the yard of our lady missionary colleagues. That took a twenty-minute walk using a shortcut through a typical noisy African market. It was ok in the dry season but not so pleasant in the wet season.

Communication was by shortwave radio, long before the days of mobile phones. But this lack of security also meant that there was no way Margaret could take the vehicle and drive herself to do her own shopping. Police would take the vehicle off her at gunpoint – a white woman driving by herself was just not viable or safe. So, what started off being a great blessing to have our own place, became a virtual prison for Margaret staying on her own when I was away for many hours at daily Bible studies. Despite that, she fully supported me in what I was doing.

She began writing a long series of Sunday School lessons in Portuguese to accompany an existing excellent set of visual aids. They proved a wonderful blessing to many Sunday

Schools and Good News Clubs and not only in Luanda. She asked a lovely lady of mixed race and proficient in Portuguese to come to our flat and help her. She and Irene Cardoso spent many happy hours writing and proofreading those lessons trying to find the best wording. There were many laughs and cups of tea as they enjoyed each other's company. The lessons were used for many years.

Margaret and Irene realised that a necessary step would be to take these teaching materials and introduce Sunday School teachers to them so that they were comfortable and capable of using them in Sunday Schools not only in Luanda but also in the provinces. The hope was that at least some of them would be able to encourage other teachers to use this material. They knew that it would take time for new material to be accepted and used confidently. So various seminars were organised in Viana. The visual aids and teacher notes were provided free of charge to all present and also made available to those taking them to the provinces. Preparing all the material had been a lengthy time-consuming process but they were totally convinced of the value of providing interesting well-illustrated material to assist Sunday School teachers to fulfil their vital role in teaching the next generation the truths of the gospel.

Irene Cardoso was later commended to full-time service to the Lord and has made incredible sacrifices to move back to Kavungu, a very remote rural area where her family once had a good farm and flourishing business. Independence had ended all that. Her father was Portuguese, and her mother Angolan.

When we visited Angola in 2015, we had an opportunity to see some of the immense range of work for the Lord she undertakes as she at the same time, tries to support herself financially. More of that later.

A seventh-floor flat without a lift had another advantage. All our provisions including lots of boxes of books and Bibles had to be carried up those stairs. In places, the railings were gone as were parts of some steps. It was a daily workout and especially so in the hot season in up to 35°C with high humidity. No problem with the so-called 'middle age spread'.

Yes, there had been a lift that worked. By that time, the doors on each landing still opened, only to reveal a gaping dark hole to the bottom. Some made use of it to get rid of all kinds of rubbish – best to leave that to your imagination. Can you imagine the danger to young children playing on the landings who had enough energy and curiosity to open those doors?

When our first dry season in the flat ended, we discovered that rain leaked into every room. A quick roof inspection revealed the problem. No maintenance had been done for years neither by the government owner nor did our rent-paying neighbours have the financial means to do anything about it other than keep a good supply of buckets and cloths.

I had no experience in the building trade but ended up importing from the UK through Medical Missionary News - which still functions - many rolls of two kinds of roofing felt that needed to be applied with a flame thrower. Enough rolls to cover three flats, half the building. If we only did our own, the runoff from the other two roofs would still penetrate into our rooms.

Realizing that this was brutally heavy work I enrolled help from two sources. Some were strong young men, sons of our neighbours whose roof would benefit. Beneath the stairs slept several young men who seemed to have nowhere else to stay, no family. Some might have been on drugs, others may have been dodging being kidnapped and put into the army, which was a normal procedure, or had run away from fighting and could not return. We got to know – well sort of know – several of these including one with a muscular physique called Americano. It was not propitious to ask too many questions. Some were decent respectful young men who had hit on hard times in a civil war. One said he had lost all his family in the war. It happened only too frequently. They didn't even ask for pay but I suspect they somehow expected that the white missionary would be generous. It was hot work in the dry season melting those layers unto the roof and a little dangerous. There was no parapet to the edge, so it took a steady head to cover the edges adequately with the flame thrower and a well-measured roll. It was seven floors up.

These young men got to know us better and respect us. We helped them with food and gospel literature and some even wanted and merited having their own Bible. Some people were terrified of them, but as we got to know them, they were only too willing to help carry groceries, etc upstairs – a bonus for Margaret. A neighbour young man, a believer, was willing to join a 'Seja' Bible Study and became an excellent student. Just recently we received a WhatsApp from him informing us that he is now married with two children, has a good job, and attends an evangelical church in Luanda.

Lesson 4
AK47s and blue bandages

Of course, being a wealthy-looking white man in an African community has its problems – now called 'challenges'. Well, anybody who could afford a nice clean undamaged Landrover had to be wealthy. One late afternoon I was being deposited at the foot of our building together with that same neighbouring young man while our vehicle was taken on to its night-time location. We had enjoyed a good Bible study.

Margaret looked out and saw the vehicle disappear so knew it would only be a few minutes until I would appear. To her amazement, there were lots of gunshots, but she assumed in a neighbouring block of flats – which was not totally unusual. We were both already able to identify the distinctive rattle of an AK47.

As I approached the stairwell in our block of flats, two men were descending the stairs in a hurry, both carrying an AK47. They grabbed my neat briefcase and since I was reluctant to lose my Bible, lots of teaching notes, and student exercise books, they both opened fire and also knocked me to the ground using the butt of a rifle. Bullets seemed to ricochet noisily in all directions. My glasses slid away and the briefcase was gone. My young Angolan friend, Dudas, was OK and quickly found my glasses. Getting up was painful as was climbing the stairs. It did take a little longer than usual and I presented a dishevelled sight at our front door.

At night in bed, I was surprised to hear a grating sound from within my body. It didn't take too long to discover that I had at least two broken ribs as well as various bruises. Descending stairs was not an option, nor could an X-ray be easily arranged. We were recommended to apply strong bandages around the chest and give the ribs peace to heal by themselves. Amazingly we had just recently received in a parcel from N. Ireland some broad strong dark blue self-adhesive elasticated bandages. We could surely be forgiven for thinking it was a mistake as we had no connection with medical work. Those bandages had been bought and packed months before somewhere in N. Ireland. The Lord knew when and where they would be needed. Otherwise, we would have had no hope of finding such things.

Of course, when I began to feel a little better, I remembered that my New American Standard Bible was gone, stolen for the second time. It wasn't only the Bible but what about all the notes written in margins over many years? Word was sent to my students of what had happened. Some said they would come to me when I couldn't go to them so that was great. I recall saying to Margaret just before a group of students arrived 'I wish I had my Bible because I know I have some good notes on this passage'.

Shortly afterwards there was a knock at the door. We were still a little nervous so as Margaret went to answer the knock, one of the students, a big lad of at least six feet, went right at her shoulder just to be sure. There was a woman who proffered an opened briefcase and asked Margaret if she recognized anything in it and added, 'Please don't ask any questions'. The briefcase wasn't mine but there was my Bible and a host of other valuable documents – ID cards, etc. Margaret gratefully accepted the briefcase and thanked the woman who promptly turned on her heel and hurried away.

Those notes in the margin were very useful. As we emptied the briefcase contents on the table, it became obvious that these documents belonged to others in the same building who had been attacked before me and their briefcases taken. One businessman in our building admitted that he had a large sum of US dollars in his briefcase -the week's takings from his thriving business.

We sent word to various neighbours. They happily identified their precious documents, thanked us, and went away. At the bottom of the briefcase was a lovely set of new shiny Toyota car keys. Someone was able to enlighten us that another neighbour had the keys to his new car in his stolen briefcase. A look over the balcony revealed an armed guard standing watch over a lovely new expensive Toyota car. The owner had taken that precaution. You can guess his delight when we sent for him and produced both his valuable documents and the keys of his car. We became friends and I had the opportunity to explain the simplicity of the gospel to him and his lady 'partner' – his wife was still alive and living elsewhere.

In a strange way, that broke the ice so that various neighbours who had previously largely ignored us got to know us, trust us and were more willing to talk giving us the opportunity to explain who we were and what we were doing there. To the inevitable question 'But what do you do?' I would frequently answer that we were in the business of helping people to get to know God and serve Him. That was usually an opener for a longer explanation of the gospel. We were even invited into some people's homes.

Wasn't the Lord gracious in not only saving my life and the lives of others but in guiding the owners of the AK47s to return vital documents and my Bible? I lost no money. As for the blue bandages, they were the Lord's timely provision.

Yes, it raised some interesting questions. Why would the bandits return a Bible and documents? Is there such a category as decent thieves? And where did the woman fit into the pattern? Luanda was offering more excitement than we really needed or wanted. Clearly, the Lord was (and still is) in complete control.

But the seventh floor flat had unexpected advantages. On one occasion when there was a considerable commotion in the city, with uproar and rioting, so that many roads were either blocked or unsafe to travel, we had such a good view of a wide section of the city that we were able to use our handheld shortwave radios to give guidance to colleagues as to which routes to avoid and which looked safer from our vantage point.

Another view that we could have done without was of celebrations. It was not unknown that when people got carried away with excitement whether when Brazil won the world cup or when a new year needed to be welcomed in with some style, hundreds of people simply took their guns and fired off shots galore ostensibly innocently simply into the air. What they seemed not to be aware of was that bullets fired into the air always had to come down somewhere. Many were killed every time it happened. Our vantage point gave us almost a bird's eye view of these white-hot bullets whizzing through the air, and I even had the presence of mind to take a picture over the edge of our balcony much against Margaret's admittedly wiser judgment.

Lesson 5
Annual Bible School and Camps

Before we arrived in Luanda, dear Marjorie Beckwith did all in her power to encourage the study and teaching of the Scriptures while at the same time recognising fully the biblical injunction for men and not women to teach the Scriptures to a mixed audience. She saw the need for an annual coming together of those interested to learn the Scriptures from men gifted and capable of teaching them. She encouraged us to visit Luanda and for me to participate in the annual Bible School held in a large well-built hall in Viana some distance out of Luanda. The excellent building was largely the result of the dedication and funding by Charlie Shorten spoken of earlier and like Marjorie from Canada.

Mostly younger men who spoke Portuguese came from whatever provinces had access to travel to Luanda. Many Chokwe's came from the more northern provinces. This Bible School would last for four weeks depending on available teachers. Hence, I was roped in.

One of the outstanding able teachers was Dr. Jayro Gonzalves, a Brazilian judge. His teaching was superbly well presented but his width of vocabulary stretched even the most fluent Angolan Portuguese speakers.

For me, it was a daunting task teaching for days on end, each morning and afternoon but those attending seemed insatiable in their desire to study God's Word. There was no idea of a 20 or30 minute sweet thought from the Bible with members of the audience closing their Bibles and shuffling their feet if you dared go over that time limit. Moreover, they longed for typed notes in Portuguese to help them re-read and then re-teach the same material back in their home Sunday Schools, youth meetings, and local assemblies. Many hours were spent duplicating notes often for more than 100 'students'. What a marvellous opportunity to teach and try to answer a multitude of questions while admitting that I didn't have all the answers. At times it was a near impossible challenge as I didn't understand the cultural backdrop of the question or questioner while taking into account that the teaching of the 'white missionary' could be quoted as authoritative for years to come. James spoke of the danger of becoming a teacher and its heavy responsibility.

That thirst for the Word was partly due to a shortage of well-taught elders and partly due to the low level of education, the result of years of civil disturbance where survival was more important than education. Healthcare and education were early invisible casualties with long-term widespread consequences. Another unexpected consequence was that many young men were uneducated whereas in some areas, young women took full advantage of any educational opportunities they could manage. That too had consequences for marriages and families.

In some sense, we were following in a well-established excellent earlier missionary tradition. Some earlier missionaries had seen the strategic importance not only of evangelism but also of regular systematic Bible teaching. David Long who was fluent in Chokwe, built a lovely small Bible School in Luma Cassai. It has a plaque with 'Escola Biblica' (Bible School) written on it to the left of the door.

There was space for about 30 desks for men who came at least once a year for several weeks when they were free from cultivating. The following year they would return for further teaching.

Other men, like Ernest Wilson had done a similar solid work of Bible teaching among the Umbundu tribe in the south-central area. Mr. Wilson's book "Angola Beloved" (out of print) has become a missionary classic though now some of the historical information is somewhat outdated. However, in his book (p238) he listed some of the topics studied in a Bible school.

'The school usually had three daily sessions of two hours each – morning, afternoon and evening. With fellow workers in the area we set out a systematic course of study to be followed. It usually conformed to the following pattern:

A New Testament book study, such as Romans or First Corinthians.

A character study, including the lives of Abraham, Joseph, David, Peter, Paul, John etc.

Doctrine: redemption, justification, sanctification and related themes.

Church: its universal and local aspects, the ordinances, worship, church government.

The Person of Christ: His deity, humanity, death, resurrection, priesthood and coming again.

There was no rigid rule about following a curriculum but we tried to teach and build up the Christians in the great truths of the faith.'

So, it comes as no surprise that we quickly discovered that many of the older believers who had been taught by David Long and Ernest Wilson and their colleagues retained a firm grasp of Bible teaching that they never forgot. The vision and dedication of those missionaries in thorough systematic biblical teaching paid rich dividends.

Another thing I gleaned from the experience of those early missionaries was how they recognized and built upon the strengths of believers from differing tribal groups. For example, when itinerating with a group of believers, Mr. Wilson liked to have some Chokwes with their traditional aggressiveness as they were excellent as evangelists in preaching the gospel but was also careful to choose some Ovimbundu to go along too as they tended to be more gifted as careful Bible teachers. So, the differing gifts blended together into a richer stronger team working harmoniously alongside the foreign missionary.

It seems to me that some believers live largely without the regular systematic carefully balanced exposition of books of the Bible over a number of years. The absence of such teaching is sometimes justified as 'the leading of the Holy Spirit'. Could it be that in reality there is no contradiction in carefully organizing systematic Bible exposition of books of the Bible and of Bible doctrine while being totally dependent on the leading, help, and guidance of the Holy Spirit?

Iris Floyd with her nursing training made use of the abundant space alongside the hall at Viana, on the outskirts of Luanda, to arrange to have constructed a teaching area and dormitory for training rural Primary Health Care workers. She worked incredibly hard with total dedication to acquire the necessary government accreditation and then teach the course with minimal assistance from a few qualified nurses. The idea was superb, trying to fill a great need of basic health-carers in rural areas denuded of nurses and doctors but with the vacuum being filled with witchdoctors and all the attendant evil of witchcraft. Where else could desperate people turn to? Sadly, the continuation of the civil war made it virtually impossible for most of those trained by Iris to return to their native villages and rural towns, so they were stuck in Luanda. There were constant struggles – to fund the needed basic equipment and drugs, how to encourage those trained to avoid simply selling basic drugs and treating patients only for profit. But it was necessary to recognise the need to allow them to earn a simple living wage. Almost all were previously unemployed. Iris worked tirelessly largely unaided in even sweltering heat and humidity and did an excellent job. She wasn't young.

That same dormitory area was also very useful for the Bible School students who came from a distance.

Likewise, the dormitory served for the girls' and ladies' camps where Margaret was asked to speak. She worked hard at having both talks and visual aids ready, often by the light of an oil lamp during the frequent power cuts – see pic. She enjoyed precious times teaching God's Word though many of the ladies displaced from rural areas spoke little Portuguese, so the messages often had to be translated, which made question and answer sessions much more difficult. She also taught new choruses and played a keyboard to accompany the singing – another helpful ability. She was always very self-effacing about her musical ability, but it was a real blessing.

Both Margaret and Marjorie enjoyed the annual girls' camps. Many girls heard the gospel clearly presented daily and some for the first time. It was really hard tiresome work in the heat of Luanda but Margaret never complained. She and Marjorie somehow managed to get some sleep in a small very hot room that was part of the building. With no electricity, the heat was most uncomfortable without a fan. Can you imagine the nightmare of logistics and feeding so many for a week and with relatively few capable trustworthy Angolan younger ladies. There were quite a few who looked up to Margaret for leadership and her clear teaching of Scripture both to unbelievers and believers.

Marjorie was renowned for her non-singing-on-key ability, but she too worked tirelessly at all the ladies' camps both teaching and sorting out endless logistics. As a nurse it was nearly impossible for her not to try to help those who needed any help within her human ability. She never spared herself even though an ageing lady.

Needless to say, for all these activities whether Primary Health Care courses, Bible School teaching or camps for ladies and camps for girls, virtually all costs had to be paid by the missionaries involved as we were working largely with IDP's – Internally Displaced People - who were without a steady income. The major exception was some of the ladies who ran small-scale stalls selling in the informal markets. A few did well financially while most just managed to scrape a basic living for their family. Women were frequently the sole family earners as most men were largely unemployed. You can imagine the internal family tensions.

Lesson 6
Malaria and medical needs

Living and working among large groups of people was all part of the package. Preaching and teaching crowds of people always risked being bitten by mosquitoes and in the wet season they were everywhere. It seemed like millions of them. They would enjoy feeding on someone else's blood and then gorge on ours. Every one of them seemed like a serious health hazard and I knew a bit about malaria already. Within our own apartment we could take lots of precautions, like sleeping under mosquito nets well tucked in all round, making sure that all windows were wholly protected with netting, but once we stepped outside our solid wooden door and then the strong metal door, it was like stepping into a mosquito war zone.

Though we took anti-malarial medication and tried to remember to cover our exposed skin with the best mosquito-repellent available (called Mosquito Milk) to deter mossies from biting our white skins, the creatures frequently won the struggle. On one occasion we both took malaria at the same time. No medication we had seemed to work. Neither of us had enough energy or even the desire to prepare food. For a day or two that was ok, but as the days wore on, we were getting weaker and had no one to help. So, we thought the unthinkable and prayed. The final recourse has to be a quinine injection into a part of the anatomy not normally exposed. I have always hated receiving injections but giving them in a medically critical situation certainly has not endeared me to the process. Margaret injected me and I injected her. No practice runs on oranges. We still have the scars on the said part of our anatomy, but it worked. At least we both have them.

You might wonder if a supply of injection syringes, needles and vials of quinine is all part of what a normal English teacher carries in his smart briefcase but marrying a well-organized pharmacist is highly recommended. The Lord had already all that under control.

The Lord saw our need of some nourishing food to help us recover strength. A kind Swiss missionary friend, Crista Bez, heard about our predicament and brought us supplies of the most deliciously enticing soup and other easily digested food. On a different but similar occasion, a lovely American lady from the Ladies Bible Study Margaret attended, discovered our situation and likewise produced the most appetising delicacies. It was amazing how the Lord so graciously and marvellously provided the right caring people at exactly the moment of need. Again, ravens didn't need to be pressed into service.

That Ladies Bible study was a monthly treat that Margaret enjoyed. The oil business had many North American believers among the engineers and technical staff. Their wives were not allowed to work for a wage so as well as dedicating themselves to charitable work they organised a Bible study in one of their homes. When I say 'homes' I mean places that were like a little piece of the USA with a level of luxury that we rarely saw in Luanda. These included some truly gracious godly ladies who knew their Bible but more importantly knew the Lord in a special way and their lives showed it. They heard about Margaret and invited her to join them. That was a tonic for her. It was all in English. She was able to contribute to their study of Scripture and made some good friends, though they seemed to come and go as their husbands moved on. Of course, it was ladies only except for the occasional special event when husbands were invited. Incidentally, those dear ladies could cook up an amazing variety of some very lovely dishes and in their kindness, they would sometimes send me a welcome 'peace offering'.

Please don't ask me why, but many Angolans seemed to think that all white people were somehow divinely gifted with medical skills even though we made it clear we had NO medical training. Still, they were frequently desperate. We often had access to drugs that in those days were sent legally from the UK. Margaret made use of her pharmacy qualification. She did pharmacy for her degree before reverting to teaching science subjects. She needed both her pharmacy and her teaching skills. Isn't it amazing how the Lord trains us with the needed skills and experience even when we aren't aware of it?

Talking of how the Lord met a variety of what could have easily and quickly turned into a medical emergency, reminds me of a certain Christmas. A Brazilian Christian couple with two lovely young children had come to live and work for the Lord in Lubango. Now Lubango is one of the most pleasant towns in Angola, situated at an altitude that gives it an almost Mediterranean climate and in a prosperous fertile farming area. They invited us to visit them, and we didn't have to be asked twice. Luanda was constantly wearing us down so brief relief was wonderful.

While visiting them in Lubango I developed a bad chest infection that worsened into pneumonia. Our Brazilian friends had a lovely comfortable bungalow on the Missionary Aviation Fellowship compound which had several houses. Dr. Collins, a Canadian medical doctor whom we already knew came to visit a family living in another of those houses. He was easily diverted to visit me and quickly diagnosed pneumonia and recommended a certain excellent strong antibiotic. But where in Angola could you find such a course of antibiotics? And it was Christmas when pharmacies were closed. Anyhow they would almost certainly not have any antibiotics. This was Angola. The doctor knew a Christian Canadian nurse who lived just a few houses away. She carried her own quite extensive stock of medicines including the exact antibiotics I needed. She was only too happy to help. So, both a well-qualified experienced medical doctor and a well-stocked Christian nurse were on hand at exactly the right time. How could anyone arrange that in the middle of Angola and over the Christmas holiday time?

On another occasion, I was the one who had the medicines needed. Let me explain. A Brazilian Christian couple came to live and work for the Lord in Luanda. They witnessed fearlessly and in a relatively short time had a considerable following and formed what seemed like a thriving local church with a large attendance. He had an enviable oratorical flow of Portuguese and a charmingly endearing personality – a lovely believing couple. He preached the gospel of salvation faithfully, but I was not impressed with him teaching these new believers that for all their medical needs the Lord would supernaturally heal them without recourse to any conventional medicines. To many, it sounded like just what was needed in a country full of penniless ill people and an almost non-existent health system – unless you could pay privately, which was fanciful for most people.

Time passed and the church kept on growing. One day he himself took malaria. Despite all he had taught he was obliged to take several anti-malarial drugs but still grew worse. Several of his church 'elders' came and prayed long and loud over him. His wife sent for me to discuss the situation. I prayed with him quietly asking for wisdom from the Lord. His worried wife had heard of a recently released new drug that was considered the best available but had no idea how or where to find it. Moreover, in the back of their minds was the certainty that for him to take such medicine would shatter his Pentecostal reputation amongst his congregation. I was somewhat surprised that his wife wondered if I could help. As it happened I had a link with Medicos sem Fronteiras (doctors without borders) in Luanda who were from Belgium. A quick visit to their premises informed me that a plane would be arriving within two days and would bring a supply of the required drug. I relayed the message.

It was a happy couple who received from me the course of treatment. By then he didn't require any persuasion from anybody to start taking the treatment immediately. We trusted the Lord to use this medication to bring healing to the dear brother in dire need. It began to work within days. When he was better, I confess I couldn't resist the temptation to tell him I was considering visiting 'his church' to testify to how the Lord had so supernaturally healed him. He nearly blew a gasket. I simply insisted that really it would cause great rejoicing that the Lord - Jehovah Jireh – provided the needed drugs. I had no intention of doing it, but he got the message. Should I be ashamed of myself? Probably, but I do confess that I enjoyed doing it.

It's not that I don't believe the Lord can heal miraculously. He can and still does, in accord with His sovereign will, but he also expects us to use what is available through the expertise and research abilities He has given to even atheistic or agnostic scientists. I have also seen what God can do supernaturally, but that's another story.

On another occasion, we saw clearly the gracious hand of God when Margaret needed an urgent medical intervention which we knew would only be available outside Angola. At that time, we needed not only a Visa to enter the country but likewise had to apply weeks in advance to leave the country with the benefit of a re-entry Visa. Looking back, it was fascinating that the Lord had put it into our minds that it was time to leave Angola to take advantage of an invitation from missionary colleagues in Harare, Zimbabwe to enjoy a short break of rest and relaxation. The stress of everyday life was getting to us. So, we decided on the date and applied some weeks well in advance for the necessary exit and re-entry Visas and were delighted when they were granted. That allowed us to book our flights. What we didn't know was that quite suddenly Margaret would develop a medical condition that needed urgent medical surgery not readily available in Angola. The timing was so precise as we had both just received our Visas and our flight tickets. If we had needed to start that whole procedure when Margaret got ill, it would have been at best a very serious situation and maybe even critical.

When we arrived at Luanda airport, it was distressing to be told that our names were not on the flight list for that journey to Harare. In those days there were no seats in the departure lounge, so we sat on our suitcases. Margaret was in considerable pain and discomfort but there was nothing we could do, humanly speaking. We prayed to the Sovereign Lord. We watched as all the other passengers were waved through while we sat on our luggage. We suspected that the airport official was waiting hopefully for a bribe once we became sufficiently desperate, but we had no intention of paying any bribes.

When all the other passengers had passed, as the last passengers we were eventually called and allowed to board the flight for which our tickets and all our other documents were completely in order.

But the Lord's gracious care continued. On arrival with our missionary colleagues, John and Eleanor Simms, they arranged that within a very few days Margaret was able to see a medical doctor who also arranged for her to see a specialist surgeon to have an operation in a nearby excellent Roman Catholic hospital. It could not have been arranged more efficiently in any country. The operation went very well, and she was lovingly cared for by the nuns.

It was fascinating to discover that the surgeon had a brother who lived in Co Down in Northern Ireland. When asked tactfully who we were and what we were doing in Angola, it was surprising that he offered to do the operation without charge if we found payment difficult. Being a firm believer that 'a workman is worthy of his hire' we assured him that we would happily pay in full. The Lord had also provided us with the additional cash needed and at the right time as part of His ongoing fatherly care. Did we ever doubt His loving timely provision for all our needs even in what seemed like an impossible medical crisis well outside human control?

Lesson 7
Containers and flights

Containers were an amazing blessing but also at times we felt overwhelmed when we were receiving one 20-foot container per month from the UK plus another few from Canada and sometimes a 40-foot one. It was hard work, expensive, and time-consuming. Was that what we had come to Angola to do?

Graduation Day at TCD
with my parents

Dad, mum, sister Mildred,
me and Rusty.

GLD team in western Ireland

Original building of Dunclug Gospel Hall.

For Information.

BALLYMENA GOSPEL HALL - Cambridge Avenue
Ballymena.

Correspondent:

T.S. Hamill,
65 Broughshane Road,
BALLYMENA.

1st October, 1979.

"Gather my saints together unto me, those that have made a covenant with me by sacrifice." Psalm 105.5.

Beloved Brethern,

A number of brethern who take an interest in the new hall at Dunclug, Ballymena expressed a desire, some time ago, to commence an Assembly in that hall. The Overseeing Brethern have accepted this proposal and have announced to the Assembly that it is left to each individual to judge for themselves where their loyalty and responsibility lies. The first meeting of the new Assembly will D.V. be Lord's Day, 7th October at 11.30.a.m.

We heartily commend this new company of believers to the Lord and to the Word of His Grace and pray that they may be guided and led in a way pleasing to the Lord.

Signed on behalf of the above Assembly.

Robert Buick   *Jim Stewart*   *Ernest Clar*

W J Stewart   *J Wallace*   *T.S. Hamill*
(absent
with leave.

Copy sent to: "ASSEMBLIES" at

Broughshane;	Clough;	Harryville;
Kells;	Ballywatermoy;	Rasharkin;
Buckna;	Ahoghill;	Clonkeen;
Crosskeys;	Antrim;	Ballymoney.

also to "Believers' Magazine with attached advertisement for insertion in same.

Letter from Cambridge Avenue elders.

Our wedding on 7th July 1972.

George and Ena Wiseman.

Ruth Hadley at her front door.

Charlie and Betty Shorten.

The missionary house, Camumdambala.

Entrance to Biula Mission station.

Team of Camp leaders.

1977 Camp. St Columba's High School, Perth, Scotland

Alf and Clella Poland

Old Lisbon street

With our landlady in Amadora

25th April Bridge, Lisbon

Emily and Eva's house, Cazombo.

Viriato and Ruth Sobral, Espinho.

Our first floor flat on RHS in Caldas da Rainha

Our minibus.

Camp at Palhal.

Sunday evening prayer time at Kalene.

Ken and Doreen Barker

Isuzu vehicle in Zambia.

Men's Bible Study group in our lounge.

Songo believers in Cacuaco, Luanda.

Victoria Falls.

Saturday morning Good News Club, Luanda

Boa Vista Bible study men.

Ladies conference at Viana, Luanda.

A typical roadside Angolan market.   Irene Cardoso and Margaret.

Training Sunday School teachers.

Building of David Long's part-time Bible School at Luma Cassai.

Roof repairs

Container work.

Making visual aids by lamplight.

Bernardo Capeio with the severely damaged Landrover

The blessing of a forklift.

Airfreighting seeds inside a cargo plane

A MAF plane.

The 3 ladies leaving Luanda for Saurimo

The kitchen Luena.

Drs Juan and Adriana Palacios, Luena.

Men's Bible Study group in Luena.

Village gospel preaching

The original 'Jesus saves' clinic in Luena.

Landmines and white stones.

A wet season road.

A village crowd listening to the Gospel.

Building the Tabernacle.

A would-be carpenter.

Matthew Jenkins, Afonso, Jonathan and Ruth Singleton at Biula.

Needy widows in Saurimo behind Ruth Hadley's house.

Our Indian friends in Kitwe

Our rented bungalow in Kitwe.

'Teacher training college Bible Study group, Kitwe.

Bible study in Kitwe School of Nursing.

A new bridge built by missionaries.

Good News Club, Kitwe.

Getting on to a good bridge.

Amano Christian School, Chingola.

Irene Cardoso and Ruth Hadley.

Elders conference in Luena.

Camundambala village primary school

Margaret teaching S.S. teachers.

It was a battle to get containers out of the grossly overcrowded port and do it within the allotted time limit otherwise a fine of $100 / about £85 a day was imposed. We had no choice but to pay a worker to do that task for us as a group of missionaries and jointly pay his wages. His name was Kaluiji meaning literally – little river. Most of the contents were supplies ordered by any of our group of 6 missionaries – Marjorie Beckwith, Iris Floyd, Margaret and me in Luanda, plus Ruth Hadley and Mary Stewart in Saurimo. That was the best way to ship medical supplies. The remainder was often used clothing in abundance.

Sometimes the port authorities were downright corrupt in how they classified incoming goods in the hope of extracting more money in taxation from the foreign missionaries or indeed of denying entry. One of the most blatant was the classification of an old diesel-engined Bedford pickup truck that had a high mileage, but we were assured by Bryan Bland at MMN that it still would be of some use. It was amazingly classified as 'a war machine' and as such could not be imported. It was fairly obvious that someone either in the port or in Customs had their eye on it as their potential new mode of transport that might also help them to enhance their income. It always came down to money.

Still, it was well worth importing and was greatly used in the Lord's work in Bié. Sadly, another attempt to assist the believers there with additional transport came to an undesirable end.

We determined that if the Lord were to provide us with adequate funds, we would purchase a new vehicle more suited to city use than a Landrover Defender and offer our still reliable vehicle to the believers in Bié. When that became possible, we went ahead and bought a Toyota Prado and offered the Landrover Defender to where it would be better suited. The Bié believers were thrilled to have such a suitable vehicle and it was promptly put to good use.

While both we and they were well aware that the risks of hitting a landmine were always real it was a disappointment when before long it hit a landmine. The engine block took the bulk of the blast thus sheltering the driver from severe injuries. The vehicle was wrecked beyond repair but in the goodness of God the driver stepped out with only relatively minor cuts and bruises.

Even driving to teach the Scriptures in local assemblies in Luanda sometimes carried an amount of unforeseen risk, like the shock of seeing live ammunition carefully piled in circles right beside the dirt path. This ammunition had been scattered over a wide area after the opposition movement successfully hit a large government ammunition dump at the airport. The initial explosions started other explosions that scattered ammunition far and wide. It was not unusual to see local children playing with live ammunition. Many were maimed, some were killed. It took a long time for the government to gather up all this ammunition and render it safe.

But I digress. Once each container was released from the port, payment had to be made to have the container transported to the storage area in Viana beside the building used for training primary healthcare workers and holding camps and conferences. While roads were open and passable, a truck had to be hired to take the needed supplies to Saurimo. The road was atrocious, especially in the wet season and trucks could get stuck in deep mud. That was not counting any security risks from opposition troops or simply bandits cashing in on the chaos. All told, each container could easily cost well over £5,000 at our end of the proceedings in Angola. The cost of shipping from the UK was generously covered by Medical Missionary News from gifts they received. Of course, getting each container cleared by Customs was another challenge. Eventually, after much negotiation, it was agreed that Customs officials would come to the Viana storage area to open and inspect that the contents were as declared. In reality, they always were, but Customs officials also had families and relations in need. Need I say more?

Was it worth it? Largely speaking abundantly yes. Without such supplies as books, Bibles, medical supplies, and medicines, much of what we as a group were attempting to do would have been much more restricted. Coming from N. Ireland we were specially privileged by the many boxes with delicious foodstuffs unobtainable within Angola. These boxes were generously made up by ladies' missionary classes throughout N. Ireland. It was also a privilege to receive enough to share with some of our colleagues. The Lord Himself will adequately reward the many dear sisters who lovingly and carefully packed parcels with what they knew we needed or wanted. They did it 'as to the Lord'.

It sometimes annoyed us when just occasionally used clothing sent was not of a desirable quality. It was hard work unloading a 20-foot container when the outside temperature could be in the high 20s or even up to 35^0 C with high coastal humidity. Inside a metal container was like an oven. We were so grateful when kind believers sent us a used forklift through MMN (Medical Missionary News). It was an amazing help for which we thanked the Lord and the generosity of His people. It never ceased to amaze and cheer us that so many gave generously in many different ways to help the Lord's work in Angola.

To be honest, most of the used clothes were of good quality and were very gratefully received and especially in areas where the civil war left many thousands destitute. There was one occasion I remember especially when we were exceedingly grateful for the large quantity of used clothing we had in storage.

Our colleague Ruth Hadley in Saurimo took malaria and was very seriously ill. At that stage, she had no one with her to help. We knew what it was like to have bad malaria, but she was alone. How we knew was that we all had daily short-wave radio contact at an agreed time morning and evening. It was so essential for all of us in a country engulfed in a civil war. It became apparent that Ruth urgently needed help. But how? The road was all but impassable and being about 1,000 klms/620 miles from Luanda, would be a tiring very slow, and quite dangerous drive. Indeed, there were times when it was completely closed by the opposition movement. It was a Sunday morning. We prayed asking the Lord for guidance and His very definite intervention. For me, there was no question of attending our usual Sunday morning Breaking of Bread meeting.

Connie who was the head of the Lutheran World Federation (LWF) was a lovely stout-hearted lady from Guyana who had been brought up in a Brethren Sunday School so knew the gospel well, but as far as we could establish had never committed her life to Christ. Only the Lord knows the heart. She had the authority and the funds to hire cargo planes to transport aid to wherever planes could fly within Angola. She had met Ruth several times and evidently respected her highly. I decided to appeal to her for help in the hope that LWF might have a cargo plane scheduled to go to Saurimo on Monday morning.

She lived in a luxurious apartment block with heavy security. I approached the first armed guard at the gate and asked to be allowed to visit the lady. No, I had no appointment. I had tried to phone her, but Sunday was her day off and her phone was unanswered. Reluctantly he allowed me to pass. A second guard right at the door to the whole block was even more cautious but succumbed when I insisted that he radio the boss with my request. She had given strict instructions that she was not to be disturbed. Eventually, he gave in. I was allowed in. Without appearing at all racist, it was always difficult for a guard to bar the way to a well-dressed white man speaking fluent Portuguese who was highly respectful but quietly insistent. He might just be someone quite important.

She welcomed me politely while she was having her toe-nails polished. She listened attentively to my story and request but there were no flights booked for Saurimo in the foreseeable future. There was a pause. I prayed silently. Remember Nehemiah? Then she challenged me to have ten tonnes of goods in the airport at 6.30 am the next morning. She would organize her team of workers to have another ten tonnes ready as well. That would be the 20 tonnes needed to fill a cargo plane. Margaret and I would also be taken on that flight. I agreed, thanked her sincerely, and took my leave. Thank you, Lord, but…

What had I done? How on earth could we have that much ready and hire a large truck to transport it all into the airport from our storage containers in Viana just like that? And on a Sunday. I assembled several young men who worked for us from time to time. Would they help? Yes, for Dona Ruth. She was rightly very highly regarded by those who knew her and those who worked for her.

We did it, deeply grateful for a stockpile of clothing that had accumulated at that time because there was no way to get it up country to where it was needed. Despite it being a Sunday, we were able to get foodstuffs, bags of cement and had room for lots of supplies and anything else we thought would be helpful to make up the desired weight.

Imagine our delight as Margaret and I got to the airport on time the next morning and shortly saw the LWF truck workers unloading their cargo onto the airport apron close to a plane going to Saurimo. What's more, neither the plane loading nor the plane hire cost us anything as LWF paid the whole bill. Could you believe it? Can God do things like that? Oh yes, easily.

It was great to arrive mid-morning at the airport at Saurimo. We hitched a ride to Ruth's house and if I remember correctly with a local R.C. parish priest whom we knew. He certainly facilitated Ruth several times as well as us. He was a very kind young man with the White Fathers religious order from outside Sligo. On one occasion we had a lovely meal with him at the parish house. The Irish Border disappeared when we got together. We refrained from discussing Irish politics north or south but enjoyed discussing Scripture. The Lord can use His divinely inspired Word. That young man had a truly kind generous heart.

With the correct medication and lots of TLC Ruth recovered slowly but surely. That's how malaria is – usually. We again praised the Lord for all He had done to facilitate our safe arrival and we rejoiced in the goodness of God which knows no limits.

Lesson 8
The convenience of air travel

It is easy therefore to grasp that with the dangers and difficulties of road travel and the frequent reminders of the ongoing war, air travel had much to endear itself to us. In rural areas burnout tanks beside the road, broken bridges, and wrecked convoys of fuel trucks near massive holes in the road left by mines were a very potent reminder, if one was needed, that war was very wasteful both of lives and scarce resources that could have been put to much better ends.

At least that Lutheran World Federation pilot knew where he was going. On another flight, we had the privilege of traveling to Saurimo on a small 10-seater United Nations plane. We could only be allocated seats if the plane was not filled by other higher priority travellers belonging to UNrelated organizations – and there were many, so it was a bit doubtful, to say the least, each time that we turned up ready to fly. We would wait patiently or perhaps impatiently hoping that all the seats wouldn't be taken.

On one occasion the pilot was a young man from S. Africa who had not flown to Saurimo before. He was supposed to know that Saurimo was encircled by UNITA troops only a short way outside the town so he had to be careful that he did not come down too low too soon as he would risk being fired on by surface-to-air missiles that the UNITA opposition had. Incidentally, the Saurimo runway was littered on both sides with wrecked planes. Not a very reassuring sight for nervous fliers.

A corkscrew descent was normal. The pilot maintained a high altitude until directly overhead the airport then he put the plane into a very steep corkscrew descent with the engine-stalling warning buzzers screaming. He was very nervous, obviously terrified. Sweat was dripping off his face. The reality was that he got his descent partially wrong so he was descending over UNITA- held territory before eventually heading towards the airport. I had a quiet word with him afterwards as he didn't know the lie of the land. He vowed he would never do this flight again. By the way, you can easily imagine that we often felt that we had left our stomach quite high up somewhere among the clouds but mercifully it eventually seemed to regain its normal place though we didn't have too good an appetite for a little while.

We were offered another free flight in somewhat different circumstances. War causes people to flee from their fields so that they cannot feed themselves and their families. Even when they manage either to settle elsewhere or return to their fields, they have neither tools nor seeds to start over again. One year there was a serious food shortage with famine looming. A Canadian missionary medical doctor, Dr.

Steven Foster, undertook a massive challenge. He succeeded in raising funding to purchase a large quantity of a variety of seeds and hoe-heads made into 10 and 15 kg bags. He purchased the seeds in Zimbabwe and had them transported to Lubango in southern central Angola.

Once in Lubango however there was no possibility of trucking the seeds to Saurimo where they were most needed. Eventually, a cargo plane was hired but he couldn't find anyone who would take responsibility to accompany the loaded plane to its destination and organize the secure storage and distribution to those in desperate need. The seeds could easily end up in the hands of armed racketeers who would corruptly charge grossly inflated prices and the poor would never see the seeds they longed for. Ruth Hadley undertook to organise the unloading, safe storage and careful distribution using trusted elders from local churches. All that was needed was someone to accompany the load and ensure a safe handover. Somehow it seemed logical for Margaret and me to volunteer, so we had the joy of sitting on top of tons of bags of seeds in the cavernous hold of a Russian Antonov cargo plane flight from Lubango to Saurimo. There were no seats, seat belts or health and safety requirements. Isn't it interesting what the Lord allows us to do?

Preaching the gospel – vitally important as it is, can be greatly enhanced by determined action to help the poor and especially when some of them are also those who profess faith in Christ. Does it come as a surprise that those who saw us directly involved in unloading seeds and hoes at the airport which they received free of charge were more disposed to come with their family circle to listen to the gospel being preached on Sunday. Both the aid and the gospel were offered freely to all who recognised their need.

Incidentally in those days, Zimbabwe was called the breadbasket of central Africa and it was, often having a substantial agricultural surplus that helped feed surrounding countries suffering food shortages. Many will realise that some reports indicate that in 2021 more than half of all Zimbabweans need to be fed by the WHO (World Health Organization – part of the United Nations). We had an opportunity to visit Zimbabwe several times. It was wonderfully peaceful, prosperous, and secure compared with Angola. To us, in those days, it seemed a delightfully successful country. There were irreligious mutterings about being nearly 'heaven on earth'. Many Zimbabweans would now tell a different story.

It appears to me that President Mugabe made good decisions in the early part of his tenure including building many lovely schools and teacher-training colleges that enabled students to become useful graduates. Later it became an internationally known scandal as he enriched himself and his family while so many of his people were without work and hungry. The blatant murder and terrorising of white farmers was a deliberate racist policy to make them abandon their farms and move elsewhere. Famine resulted and still persists as the few corrupt leaders blame everyone else without considering their own complicity in their badly thought-out decisions. Could it be that what some label 'terrorists' while others call them 'freedom fighters' make good soldiers who know how to cripple an economy but seem to have less competence in making economically well-informed decisions that bring prosperity to their people? Too many people end up going hungry and emigrating legally or illegally to surrounding countries. Thousands die prematurely.

If I may be allowed another personal viewpoint, it seems to me that President Mugabe's first wife, known as Sally, had a good influence on her husband and while she lived, he made many moderate wise decisions that enriched his people. After she passed away in 1992 he remarried a much younger woman whose main interest seemed to be financially enriching herself, shopping worldwide for expensive luxury goods, and even developed a determined political ambition to succeed her husband. You can gather that I have strong views on the inestimable value of a good wife and even better, a godly wife.

One other flight deserves a mention. Missionary Aviation Fellowship does an amazing job in countries where missionary travel is all but impossible. Where roads and railways are more or less adequate, their planes are not needed. We were thrilled that they were able to establish a base in Angola, initially in Luanda then later in Lubango. In Luanda they were offered hospitality in basic rooms of an annex behind the house in Cassenda where Iris Floyd and Marjorie Beckwith lived and served the Lord and His people.

Occasionally when Ruth Hadley's supplies in Saurimo, including food, were running very low and she was urgently needing to be restocked, we asked MAF for a flight of cargo. The small single-engined plane could take a maximum of 1 ton with one passenger. It was very expensive, costing us about as much as a return flight to the UK but sometimes it was a dire necessity. On one occasion, I was the passenger.

Partway through the flight, the pilot (not the one in the picture) got very drowsy. Eventually, he asked me if I knew how to fly a small plane. The question seemed ridiculous to me, but he insisted that he was so tired and sleepy but assured me that he would be ok if only he could have fifteen- or twenty-minutes sleep. So, he gave me a quick lesson on all the instruments and controls allowing me to try out some gentle manoeuvres. It seemed relatively easy. 'Just fly straight and maintain altitude' was the simple instruction. That sounded doable.

So, I was in charge and he, very foolishly as I saw it, placed his confidence in my transition from a diesel Landrover

Defender to a Cessna Caravan single-engine plane. Not even similar. He appeared to sleep well for most of those fifteen minutes. Then I noticed billowing clouds coming closer, so decided that I was out of my comfort zone. Mercifully, he wakened refreshed, and we completed the flight uneventfully. Look what I would have missed if I had stayed in teaching in Ballymena. Flying a single-engine plane is such fun! Other flights were not fun at all.

Like flying in a Russian Antonov cargo plane loaded with badly hurt soldiers on IV drips tied to the inner part of the plane's structure. Military planes carrying troops and military equipment towards the battle lines of course had to return to Luanda. The military officers in charge quickly hit on an effective way of filling the plane and making a handsome supplement to their wages. In a sense, it would be a shame for a plane to return to base empty when so many were desperate to fly. Frequently all roads were closed. It was a kind of public service – at a price, but there were no fixed prices. To the troops, most foreign missionaries seemed to be wealthy as they usually drove good vehicles.

We needed to travel. Once we paid, our ticket was merely a scruffy piece of paper with a number on it. Sometimes we had minor qualms as we thought about bribery and corruption but usually left those discussions for the academically gifted to debate in more comfortable surroundings.

There never was any guarantee that we would both get on. Climbing aboard was something else. A locally made rough and ready not very substantial metal ladder hung vertically from an entrance. Sometimes the bottom of the ladder didn't quite touch the ground. Needs must. The challenge was to climb up with your baggage without anyone being allowed to assist. Margaret braved it like the rest, and we entered. The cargo plane had no seats, of course, so you picked where you fancied to set your baggage and sit on it and be thankful.

Take-off and landing could be interesting with nothing to hold on to.

I digress to mention a fellow missionary who described a very similar experience except that he was sharing the bare cargo hold with a sizeable flock of sheep. If you have any idea of the effect noisy take-off and landing would have on nervous sheep, then I think I can happily leave the rest to your imagination.

Back to our journey on the Russian plane. A sideways glance revealed a young man sitting beside his motorbike lying on its side. A brief sniff suggested leaking petrol and sure enough, there were drops falling on the floor. Before take-off the Russian pilot was doing a brief inspection of his cargo, heading in our direction while smoking a foul-smelling cigar. A spark or maybe a lighted cigar was all that was needed for the plentiful petrol fumes to do what petrol fumes do. We prayed hurriedly. As he approached, he suddenly turned away just in time. Thank you, Lord. Why should missionary life be dull?

Another flight from Luanda to Saurimo was memorable for a very different reason. Ruth Hadley and Mary Stewart had managed to drive from Saurimo to Luanda for Christmas, the first time since the ceasefire had been declared between the two warring parties in the civil war since 1991. The windscreen of Ruth's Landrover had been stolen from her vehicle while parked in her yard in Saurimo and there was none available in Saurimo but could be obtained in Luanda having been bought and flown in from Namibia on a MAF flight. The ladies drove without sleeping all day and all night arriving safely but exhausted in Luanda at about 4.00 am on Boxing Day very red-faced and pasted with flies and bugs despite headscarves covering most of their faces. Wisely they had brought two young men with them for security.

The new windscreen was fitted. A recently imported new Landrover Defender pickup was also ready to go to Saurimo, so both vehicles were fully loaded - and maybe slightly overloaded. The decision when to drive back to Saurimo was heavily influenced by Ruth's conviction that after Christmas most years there was usually about a week of dry weather before the tropical rains started again. In that period the deepest puddles in the roads would be somewhat less difficult and some stretches considerably less tricky. So the decision was made.

But that was exactly the days when a conference for men had been arranged in Luanda a long time ahead and I was asked and had agreed to teach the Scriptures. I was torn two ways. I didn't want to go back on a promise to speak at the conference, but I also wanted to accompany my wife and our lady colleagues on the long and always somewhat dangerous drive of about 1,000 kilometres from Luanda to Saurimo. A male accompanying three white ladies might be an advantage.

So we agreed that I would remain in Luanda to fulfil my commitment to teaching at the conference while the three ladies would rotate drivers on the return trip back to Saurimo. After the conference, I would fly on a MAF flight to Saurimo. It wasn't really what I wanted to do.

Here Margaret continues the story.

AN UNFORGETTABLE JOURNEY

It was early morning shortly after dawn that we said our goodbyes to Eric, Iris Floyd, Marjorie Beckwith, and the workers at the missionary home in Cassenda, Luanda and we all prayed that the Lord would protect us and guide us all the way to Saurimo. We little knew how much we needed that protection and that God would graciously keep us from all the dangers and evil ahead of us.

The road, they told us, was in a very bad state, bridges had been blown up and makeshift wooden logs loosely lashed together were all that was left to cross some of the rivers. In places, they had been obliged to drive through the bush to avoid parts of the road where land mines had not been lifted. These stretches were just through dry mud but deeply rutted by large trucks that had passed that way in the wet season. Our vehicles would not get through these difficult tracks once the rains would start again.

Ruth and I drove in the first vehicle with its newly fitted windscreen. Mary was right behind us in the new Landrover pickup with its canvas canopy over the back section. Both vehicles were packed full of vital supplies of medicine, food, tools, Bibles, and books, along with parcels from the ladies' missionary classes in the UK. Nothing was available to buy in Saurimo as shops were empty since the war had stopped almost all movement on the roads.

We soon left the outskirts of Luanda and passed through police and army roadblocks without any difficulty. The road surface deteriorated quickly thereafter and long stretches seemed to me to be like road works that never ended as there was no sign of tarmac and only hard beaten earth with razor-sharp stones sticking up through it – the result of tanks passing over it in the previous years. Stretches of dirt road were smooth enough and on these stretches we made good progress. As we got further inland we passed through almost deserted towns showing severe bomb damage and travelled on to forested mountainous areas where there were steep-sided ravines plunging down from the side of the road to rivers below. After that we descended to the level plains of the high plateau.

We stopped at times to rest, have something to eat and drink and change drivers. At the last of these breaks, we noticed a small pickup go past us. It was well loaded with passengers and lots of bags of maize meal - food for their families. When we started off again it was my turn to drive the first Landrover with Ruth beside me. It was late afternoon and soon we passed that little pickup which had to travel rather more slowly than us as it had such a heavy load. Ruth remarked that we must be coming near Malange where we were to stop for the night as she saw a forested area some distance ahead. A small car was ahead of us on the road, driving slowly and I made several attempts to pass it but each time the car speeded up, not allowing me to overtake so eventually I decided to just follow it. We could see that there were two men in it. By this time we were approaching the forest and as we entered it and rounded a bend we could see ahead that a truck was stopped just a short distance off the side of the road with a number of men standing beside it, all of them in some kind of military uniform.

The men in the car in front of us waved at the 'soldiers' and they waved back and signaled to all of us to move on through. We sighed with relief that we hadn't been obliged to stop at yet another military checkpoint. Without further incident, we drove on and entered the large town of Malange. There we saw the car with two men that we had followed through the forest disappear down a side road. We wondered who they were as they didn't seem to be Africans. Eventually, we reached the home of some Christians where we were to spend the night. It was a well-built semi-detached house. We received a warm welcome from the family who gave us something to eat and then showed us to their best bedroom. We made several attempts that evening to phone our colleagues back in Luanda to let them know of our progress, but without any success.

We had a reasonable night's rest and our hosts prepared us an amazing breakfast of steak and chips which we thoroughly enjoyed. Just as we were packing up to go on the next leg of our journey, at the front of the house we found a group of concerned Christians talking excitedly. They spoke to Ruth in Chokwe and she translated for me, telling the story of how there had been an ambush by bandits on the forest road last evening. They had stopped a small truck loaded with food which they stole and then killed everyone in it. We were appalled to hear that news as we well remembered the little truck which we had passed and sorrowfully thought of the poor people in it who had been murdered. We believe that God had provided an escort of two men who went before us and stayed close to us through that ambush area. They saw to it that we and our two highly valued vehicles with all their cargo passed through safely, while just a few minutes later others lost their lives at that same place. Were they men or angels? We were humbled to see God's obvious protecting care over us even when we didn't know that we were in such serious danger.

Eric.

So during the men's conference in Luanda, news trickled through that a heavily loaded vehicle had been attacked as it approached Malange and all the passengers were shot dead. The timing seemed highly probable. It was with a heavy heart of uncertainty that I continued the Bible teaching at the conference. Was Margaret in that vehicle? There was no way to check.

Margaret.

With heavy hearts, we said our farewells to the kind Christians and made our way back onto the main road towards Saurimo. About twenty miles later we saw a large truck coming towards us with a number of men on the back who were waving their arms in greeting. As they came alongside and stopped, we recognised a few of the men who were believers that we knew well in Luanda. That's where they were going. We all got out and after greeting, asked them kindly to go as soon as they could to the missionary house in Luanda and reassure our colleagues that we were all safe and well and that the Lord had saved our lives. They agreed heartily and did as they promised, bringing great relief and comfort to our dear ones waiting at Cassenda who had heard the news of the ambush and murders on the road to Malange. They knew we were travelling about that time. How gracious of God who allowed us to meet these friends who were able to confirm that we were all safe and well.

We seemed to be making good progress until a couple of hours later we came to a stop where a large, heavily loaded truck was stuck fast with a front wheel sunk hopelessly in a deep pool of mud. As it blocked the road there was no way we could get around it. Lots of the people who presumably had been travelling in the truck were amazed to see three white women in two Landrovers in the same predicament. Who would ever be able to move that truck?

Ruth and I thought it might be possible to pass on one side of the mud hole by going further up onto the ditch. So she set off. She was doing quite well until she drew level with the deep hole. Suddenly the Landrover lurched precariously into the hole and was thoroughly stuck. What were we to do? We prayed and prayed trusting that God would somehow intervene and make a way of escape for us so that we wouldn't have to spend the night on the roadside. Stranded like us, the truck's passengers were sympathetic to us. After about three hours we heard the noise of a heavy vehicle coming from the opposite direction and to our amazement, there was a large track-laying digger. The driver was willing to help and first pulled out Ruth's vehicle and then attached a chain to the big truck and pulled it off to the side of the road, allowing the traffic to start moving again. This was in a remote area with no landline phones. It was before the days of mobile phones and we were beyond the range of handheld short wave radios. It was all of the Lord's doing that we were rescued so quickly and neither vehicle was damaged. How we praised Him for His loving care and provision in answer to our feeble cries for help. Of course, many others in Angola and overseas were praying for us on that journey.

Due to this delay, it was already getting late long before we had reached our next overnight stopping place and we knew that it was unsafe to be travelling in the dark. We decided that we should stop at the next village and ask permission to pull our vehicles off the main road to stay for the night. They agreed as they were able to understand Ruth when she spoke to them in Chokwe, although they were of a different tribe. We caused great excitement as they gathered around while we made some tea and had our bread rolls to eat. Ruth overheard them say 'They're eating cake'. She told them we were missionaries and explained the Gospel simply to them and prayed with them. They had never heard it before. We returned to our vehicles to try to rest. None of us managed to sleep that night, between being much too hot with the windows closed or bitten by mosquitos when the windows were open.

As it was getting near dawn, we continued our journey and headed for Saurimo, determined to try to get there as early in the afternoon as we could. The road was considerably better, though we had to cross five or six rivers with no proper bridges. As we looked down we saw lorries and their containers lying where they had fallen into the riverbeds. We had to cross those same bridges.

By early afternoon we reached Saurimo with great thankfulness to God for a safe journey. The Christians, who hadn't heard from Ruth and Mary since they set off for Luanda, were so relieved to see them back safely and gave us all a great welcome. We managed to make radio contact with our friends in Luanda to assure them we were home safely. As we unpacked, we saw large rain clouds gather and before nightfall, there was the first rain storm. We had made it just in time. How we praised our faithful God who had been with us all the way.

Eric.

Three things stood out for us.

First, who were the men in the small car that held Margaret back from overtaking despite her best efforts in a much faster vehicle? Do angels drive saloon cars in Angola?

Second, in the goodness of God that brother was on the truck that saw the missionary ladies the day after the killing of the passengers in the next vehicle. They saw them, talked with them and also knew me and where I was living.

Third. The 'soldiers' were bandits but why did they allow the three missionary ladies to pass unharmed despite them driving two very fully loaded Landrovers coming immediately behind the men to whom they waved? When they were eventually caught and taken to court, they pleaded for mercy in that as they put it 'we spared the three madres' – 'madres' being their name for Roman Catholic nuns.

The three ladies arrived safely in Saurimo before the rains recommenced and I joined them later on the much more comfortable MAF flight after the conference finished. We had a good time around God's Word and the Lord gave me the needed grace to continue despite my turmoil of mind in uncertainty about Margaret's safety. Trusting the Lord is easy in theory. Another practical lesson.

Chapter 7
VISITS TO ANGOLAN PROVINCES

Luena in Moxico Province

Although we were confined to Luanda we decided to try to respond to the many requests from various provinces to visit and teach a mini-Bible school for a week or two. Luena in Moxico Province was one place that we enjoyed visiting for about two weeks at a time. For one thing, we could fly to Saurimo and stay a few days with Ruth Hadley knowing that she would drive us in her Landrover to Luena. While I taught the men, Ruth and Margaret would teach the women and children. It was amazing that in the middle of all the shortages, difficulties, and danger, over a hundred men would attend day after day for the simple straightforward exposition of Scripture.

On several occasions we stayed in what had once upon a time been a small well-cared-for one-bedroom apartment occupied by a single English missionary lady, Elizabeth Davis. It was behind the Portuguese concrete well-constructed town-centre building for the sole Portuguese-speaking assembly. Both the spacious hall and the accommodation behind it were built when a missionary, Clifford Beggs was in Luena. When we arrived, the accommodation was just an empty shell with a door that more or less closed but had neither running water, electricity, furniture nor curtains. Since Ruth had brought us from Saurimo in her Landrover she also made life easy for us by bringing the essentials – camp beds, the all-important mosquito nets and bedding, pots, cutlery, and a good supply of tinned food. Very little was available in Luena. We cooked on a typical African charcoal brazier outside. Water was brought to us from the river by ladies carrying calabashes or buckets on their heads. The 'kitchen' was fully equipped with two 40-gallon/200-litre metal drums for water and two rusty metal railway sleepers for shelving. Sheer luxury. It was dry season so there were no problems with holes in the roof. Who could want for more?

It was amazing the faithfulness of a dear brother who had been entrusted to look after a large trunk with some basic items in it that Ruth Hadley had left for safekeeping to facilitate her future visits. Even through the years of extreme austerity, he kept that trunk and contents safe unopened, and unused. That would have tested any of us, knowing what was in it and through years of war with an incomprehensible level of shortage of just about everything. On top of all that, there was no guarantee that any missionary would ever return. Only the Lord can fully reward such faithfulness to Him and to us His servants in respect of a trust given, accepted and fulfilled.

What a privilege it was to teach the Scriptures day after day to men thirsty to hear. There was always time left after each teaching session for questions before dark. That was a vital part that showed what they had understood and what was still unclear or even what some didn't really want to understand. It was so vital to try to clarify what Scripture says, what it means and what are the implications for each one of us. I usually tried to have with me enough copies of my notes in Portuguese so that they could take them away to mull over. I suspect there was many a long evening of lively discussion of what the white missionary said or maybe even what they thought the white missionary had said or should have said.

One great blessing in Luena was the dedication of a small team of godly men in keeping going the Emmaus Bible Correspondence Courses in Portuguese and Chokwe. They were a tremendous blessing down through the years. We never ceased to admire the commitment and exceptional dedication of the few local Angolan brothers who so sacrificially distributed, marked and corrected these excellent courses all year round. It was obvious at question times those who had carefully studied those courses as they had a grasp of Scripture that was so evident compared with those who hadn't. Of course, the Emmaus Bible studies in Portuguese were only accessible to those who had a good grasp of written Portuguese, but a good number had also been translated into Chokwe, the predominant local tribal language.

As the war dragged on and came ever closer to Luena, more and more refugee believers came to town, many speaking Chokwe as their mother tongue. There was an almost constant struggle to build new or bigger halls to house the influx. Some that we visited would have had 400 or more believers and there were at least a dozen assemblies.

The need for Bible teaching was tremendous. As in so much of Africa, it was always relatively easy for professing believers to merge many of their pagan pre-Christian habits and cultural practices with the little they really understood of biblical Christianity. The cultural tribal rituals were so ingrained in them, especially around the areas of conception, birth, marriage, illness, alcohol, death and burial. It was always a challenge to try to help them disentangle relatively neutral tribal customs from much more serious witchcraft-related pagan practices. For any foreigner, it is always a sensitive area to comprehend what is truly behind some cultural customs to establish if they truly are neutral or are they still heavily tinged with an anti-Christian worldview. Confidence in witchcraft is insidiously prevalent at so many levels. It is such a different all-pervasive worldview. One of the books that I found most insightful was 'Free Indeed from Sorcery and Bondage' by Marvin S Wolford, a book that would be helpful for anyone contemplating living and working in any missionary capacity in central Africa. He spent over 40 years in what is now called the Democratic Republic of Congo. Others may already have observed that some countries with the word 'democratic' in their name may in reality be far from democratic.

Of course, it took and takes the ladies to deal with matters best left to them. It was so helpful when some of the older ladies had been well taught and were unashamed to expose some of the delicate private issues that could easily be hidden, glossed over, or simply not mentioned. The impact of well-respected older truly godly women can never be overestimated. By contrast, the influence of older women still clinging privately to witchcraft-related totally unbiblical practices would be corrosive in any assembly both then and now.

When we first visited Ruth in Saurimo, many of the assemblies were in a sad state. Two leading 'elders' were not so much respected as feared. They had manipulated themselves into leading administrative roles but even on slight acquaintance it soon became evident that they were involved in witchcraft and were frighteningly evil men totally opposed to the preaching of the gospel and the teaching of the Scriptures. From first sight one even struck me as looking evil. They had caused much trouble and would continue to do so while they lived. It was made a special matter of prayer both by some in Saurimo and farther afield. Mercifully there was one small assembly with godly elders who were not intimidated and believed in the power of prayer. This opposition to Ruth and all she stood for caused much sorrow and heartbreak.

Eventually the Lord graciously answered those prayers in that within a relatively short space of time both men died.

Amongst some believers there was quiet rejoicing. That they had managed to manipulate themselves into important local leadership positions clearly illustrated an ongoing spiritual danger.

Godly gracious men know how to restrict themselves to a purely minimal administrative role when so demanded by the government, but ambitious power-seeking men abuse their administrative role and become self-appointed local dictators imposing their own unbiblical ideas on what should be assemblies governed by their own true local shepherd-elders in happy co-operation with other believers.

Can you imagine our surprise on one rural expedition when we discovered a sizeable patch of marijuana, and it was being cultivated right outside the home of an 'elder'? Some might wonder how missionaries come to recognize marijuana plants. Tragically, for him it seemed critical to maintain this profitable income to support his family.

In another area, it was intriguing to discover that at least one elder's family was supported financially by the making and selling of illegal liquor. In Ireland, it would be called 'poteen' made from potatoes. Presumably it was made by the elder and sold by his wife. But both irregularities highlighted a serious problem in many larger assemblies even with godly elders, namely the lack of financial support for men who devote themselves to the study and teaching of Scripture and time-consuming pastoral care. Most have to be self-supporting financially. That can be either a tremendous blessing as the continuation of the work is not dependent on any funds from abroad or it can be an extremely heavy burden and especially for wives who do most of the cultivation to support a family.

On another visit to Luena, the believers were keen to offer us improved accommodation. A local government official was also a member of an assembly. Of course, in those days all members of local government were normally members of the communist party. She and her husband had a comfortable apartment. Evidently, well-placed or well-connected government party members were allocated or permitted to acquire or rent the well-constructed former Portuguese houses. So, on that visit, we had pleasant accommodation and good basic food prepared for us. We were treated kindly. We deemed it wiser to appreciate the kindness shown and as usual, steer clear of all political comments. The lady in question also asked no potentially incriminating questions.

In passing it might be helpful to comment that it seems to me that Africans in general and Angolans in particular, have an ability to roll with the punches. They may not necessarily be rabid communists but are willing to serve in a local communist government working for the betterment of their own people while paying at least convincing lip service to the prevalent political ideology. Astute self-preservation with a few perks thrown in often seems to be desirable.

I have also observed that some conclude it is good practice to say whatever the missionary would like to hear so as not to miss out on any help or favours that might be helpful to the family. 'Rice Christians' may not all be entirely confined to rice-growing areas of S.E. Asia.

In Luena, we were amazed at the tenacity and utter determination of the believers in desiring to have their own clinic or mini hospital to care for the thousands of believers in the town and the surrounding area. Government medical facilities were extremely limited and medical training left much to be desired. So, despite the war and with neither cement nor blocks available, they went out into the bush where they cut blocks out of termite mounds. That in itself is hard work because bricks made from 'salalei' is almost as hard as a concrete block. Then the women carried the heavy blocks on their heads along a very uneven bush path to the road where the blocks were stacked up until they had enough to fill a borrowed or rented army truck. And as they worked on the large building, they prayed that the Lord would send them a doctor and some nurses. I admired their courage and determination but wondered to myself both about their wisdom – the building they were building was huge – and what was the likelihood of any Christian doctor coming to such a remote place as Luena. My faith was smaller than theirs, but I had enough sense not to discourage them in any way despite my private reservations.

Some years passed before the arrival of a very well-qualified Christian doctor and wife team, the wife an experienced gynaecologist. They were Spanish-speaking Argentinians but had spent some time in Portuguese-speaking Brazil. They were open to visiting Luena to assess the situation and so Drs Juan and Adriana Palacios decided that that was where the Lord would have them serve Him and the local community. Not only so but they opened the way for a team of nurses to join them and another medical couple as well. Over the years the 'Jesus Saves' clinic has been enlarged and improved with the addition of more buildings. It has served the community, both believers and non-believers exceedingly well.

One fascinating result has been that Adriana's medical training combined with her kind-hearted excellent expertise as a gynaecologist has won the trust and respect of just about all the many young Muslim women having babies. On one visit I was quite surprised to find a corridor filled with veiled young women waiting to be attended. Their husbands seem to be all quite canny businessmen, but they so appreciate the care of the doctors that they have voluntarily offered to help them in surprising ways. All or almost all the bakeries in Luena are or were then run by Muslims. Dr. Juan was regularly given, free of charge, a big bag with all the bread he required and enough to give away generously to those in need.

It has been a great practical lesson on the need for both believing faith combined with 'works'. God has richly honoured their prayers and helped them with all the hard work. Many hear the gospel as a result of the 'Jesus Saves' clinic in Luena and Dr. Juan is an excellent and enthusiastic Bible teacher. Juan and Adriana have a special place in their life and ministry for young people and young couples whom they warm-heartedly welcome into their home. They both have an incurably lively sense of humour – a decided advantage.

Dundo

On our various visits to Saurimo, Ruth Hadley encouraged us to accompany her on visits to outlying areas that needed to hear the gospel preached and that could also benefit from Bible teaching. One such area was Dundo, a very rich diamond mining region where many men found well-paid employment. It also had many believers. On our way, we stopped in a village that had a hall where the believers normally met but it was relatively small. Rather than try to pack too many people into a small stuffy overheated hall, it seemed to me a better idea to make use of the strong roof rack on the Landrover. So we shuffled some of the luggage around to make enough space for two people to stand as we had taken a capable brother with us from Saurimo, Lucas Kamwamba, who could translate for me from Portuguese into Chokwe.

So, to the amazement of the onlookers, we climbed the ladder at the back of the Landrover and opened God's Word to explain the gospel of God's forgiveness, faith in Christ and a changed life with new hope for eternity after death. It didn't take long for a crowd to build up, possibly intrigued by the unexpected arrival of some 'chindele' – white faces. It was a wonderful opportunity to explain why we had come and to preach the gospel to an amazingly quiet attentive crowd all around the Landrover. When we had finished our message, it was explained that those genuinely interested should talk further with any of the elders present associated with the nearby local assembly.

To me, it was amazing that so many would listen respectfully to the preaching of the gospel and it reinforced the perception that many in Angola were quite prepared to listen to the preaching of the gospel but 'how shall they hear without a preacher?' It was absolutely marvellous that so many Angolan evangelists had spread the gospel over wide areas at immense personal sacrifice and expense as well as committed ex-pat missionaries who had worked hard for years, some for a lifetime in schools and clinics, teaching literacy, bringing loving medical care and preaching the gospel. Yet there was still the need and the opportunity for foreign missionaries to preach and teach freely. On balance possibly the greater need was for Bible teaching and Bible teachers.

Saurimo

Probably the inland town we visited most was Saurimo where Ruth Hadley and Mary Stewart, a pharmacist, lived and worked. Mary had previously worked as a pharmacist at Kalene Hospital in Zambia where I was so seriously ill. It was Mary that the Lord reminded about a small supply of the drug that could help me to stop vomiting and begin the process of recovering from malaria. Later she felt she should move across to Saurimo to accompany Ruth and do what she could to help with medical matters that were not included in Ruth's training as she was a history teacher who also enjoyed

PE and sport. She had been an enthusiastic hockey player and had played for her county.

Our visits to Saurimo served various purposes even while Mary worked alongside Ruth but were even more valuable to Ruth after Mary returned permanently to the UK. We longed for respite from the coastal heat and humidity of Luanda not to mention the chaotic traffic. We enjoyed each other's company. We would often tackle odd DIY jobs that she had neither the time nor energy to tackle.

On one early visit, it became quickly evident that she had little or no shelving and the floors had a limited capacity. It was not unknown for various car parts, new or used, to be sitting somewhere on a living room sideboard. But where could any kind of shelving be found in Saurimo where it was a major struggle even to find the basics like water and food?

A sawmill still functioned and there was a plentiful supply of good timber. So rough-sawn planks were bought. I have always enjoyed working with wood, maybe an inherited liking acquired from two uncles, one of whom was a joiner, the other a skilled cabinet maker. All that was needed then was a supply of bricks from various destroyed or derelict buildings. When the bricks were nicely cleaned of all their mortar, they made an excellent support between the shelves. It was a case of using what was available. Those shelves served their purpose for many years even though they were never stained or varnished.

Another job had to be tackled early on. Ruth wisely had installed a Lister-Petter diesel generator as the municipal supply often failed for extended periods of time or was simply unreliable both in availability and voltage quality. The voltage was so variable sometimes that it would sizzle electric equipment never mind anything electronic like a computer. Of course, a diesel generator was a heavy piece of machinery so with lots of serious vibration, it had begun to sink slowly but surely into its inadequate concrete base. Could we help?

The success of making a reinforced base for the 5 Kva generator that was permanently stable somehow may have given the impression that other jobs might be do-able.

Plumbing was a challenge. The town water supply had long since ceased to function so Ruth had to buy water from a man who sold it from a tanker which in this country would be thought to be a milk tanker. We got to thinking that in the wet season rainfall was both regular and heavy. So, it seemed logical to have large plastic barrels sent out from the UK together with some 3.5 centimetres plastic piping. The run-off from the roof was channelled into the interlinked barrels to give a reservoir of over 600 litres of relatively clean water. Of course, all water had to be carefully passed through a Swiss Katadyn 10-litre drip filter. Remembering to fill it regularly was just another of those routines that had to be learnt and observed faithfully. The alternative was to risk serious intestinal problems.

For the dry season when it doesn't rain for at least 6 months, it made sense to dig a large hole in the front garden and build a concrete tank which allowed a pump to be installed, powered by the generator. That was a big step forward as water could be stored in a raised tank. On one visit I was curious to see if I could somehow clean out the existing piping so that the water could flow into the house to the bathroom and kitchen. Previously it was a matter of keeping buckets of water topped up. After much puffing and blowing with various foot pumps it was such a joy to see very muddy rusty water oozing slowly through. When missing pipes were supplemented with some surplus green garden hose and an assortment of clips it was considered a major plumbing triumph and survived to function for many years. Another Heath Robinson DIY job.

After many years of very basic rough living, it was such a luxury for Ruth to have a bath that could be freed up from just storing water to actually functioning as a bath. In time an electric water heater was installed to supply both the kitchen and the bathroom. Later Jonathan Singleton from England was able to build a proper shower.

He and his wife Ruth have paid many extended visits to Angola sometimes staying for more than a year. He is a farmer with all the invaluable skills that a farmer must have – car mechanic, plumber, electrician, builder, plasterer. Basically, he has done any work needing to be done. Not only do we have the highest regard for his willingness to skilfully tackle just about any job but that is even more amazing when we realise how many health problems he and his wife both handle without even a hint of complaint. It seems almost incredible that such people are sometimes falsely overlooked as not being true missionaries.

I briefly mention another task Margaret and I tackled more out of sheer necessity than anything else. After attending the usual Sunday morning meetings where I was also asked to speak, Ruth made an apparently casual remark about the toilet not flushing normally. She had a suspicion about the septic tank. So it was that we started uncovering and opening the septic tank on a Sunday afternoon, a little unsure if it was highly recommended as the right way to spend a Sunday afternoon. Did the Lord not say something about pulling a sheep out of a ditch on the sabbath? Would unblocking a septic tank on a Sunday afternoon have a sound theological justification? Probably not, but we succeeded anyway. The details are best left unsmelt and unwritten.

So, in Angola and many other countries, missionary work is not all about preaching and teaching groups of people whether large or small. Those who have practical skills can offer tremendously appreciated help whether for a short time or on a longer-term basis. Brass Tacks can helpfully match volunteers to needs. If they have the ability to preach and teach as well, then that's a bonus. Such practical help is highly sought after and especially by single lady missionaries. Rest assured that the best available food will be sacrificially supplied with as many trimmings as can be obtained.

Of course, all such practical activity is during the daytime. On many late afternoons, it would be my privilege to teach the Scriptures in local assemblies. It was thrilling to see people attend these studies before they had time to go home for their evening meal after their town work or after working from early morning in their fields. Most had to walk but as time went on some had bicycles and even later, some had a motorbike.

It gave me special joy when there were opportunities to teach young men who were reasonably fluent in Portuguese. One such occasion was to an enthusiastic group of young men in Saurimo who had completed a good many Emmaus Bible Correspondence Courses so they were committed to serious Bible study. These studies were held in part of the Emmaus Bible School building which Ruth had arranged to have built to house that ever-growing work. Some of these men explained that they were having difficulty understanding what the Tabernacle was all about both to the Jews of Old Testament time and its relevance to us modern-day Gentile believers. Ruth from somewhere managed to unearth a sizeable plastic model of the Tabernacle and we were all set for an enjoyable series of Bible studies in Portuguese. With the added advantage of having listened to Prof David Gooding expound both the meaning and the modern application of the Tabernacle it was an interesting challenge to put some of that across to a Portuguese-speaking Angolan audience. Adequate time had to be set aside for questions and they were many. But what a marvellous visual aid for teaching the vital interconnectedness of the Old Testament shadows and their perfect fulfilment in Jesus Christ in the New Testament. It was well worth the effort and the students seemed to thoroughly enjoy the studies.

How privileged we are in the UK and in N. Ireland to have so many gifted godly Bible teachers and a vast array of excellent books in our own English language not to mention what is now accessible online.

On another occasion, it was my privilege to be asked to teach a series of Bible studies in a large hall in Saurimo where numbers increased steadily to well over one hundred. That time most of the week-long series was in essence answers to lots of Bible-based questions that young men had asked me on various visits to Saurimo. These included how to cope with the increasingly pervasive Pentecostal teaching on speaking in tongues as a sure sign of the filling of the Holy Spirit. A second request was about the so-called 'Prosperity Gospel' promising health, wealth and prosperity as being an incontrovertible part of God's salvation for every believer. In a land where witch doctors were known for their ability to speak in something that was amazingly similar to the Pentecostal 'speaking in tongues' and where there was no freely available functioning effective health service these were relevant pressing questions needing a biblical answer. For many believers in privileged western countries with a good health service, it is hard to conceive of the strength of the temptation for a believer to take an ailing child to a witch doctor in the hope of saving his life. What would a loving mother not do to save the life of her child? Daily pressure from unbelieving relatives makes it worse.

That Ruth returned from Luanda and remained in Saurimo throughout the many years of civil war is an amazing story of the grace of God and the indomitable courage of a young woman totally dedicated to serving the Lord by serving His people through the tough times. Let me recount two events she referred to in our many conversations together.

Not too long after her initial arrival at Biula Mission Station, a young couple, Peter and Louise Daley from USA, had arrived after her but were unable to remain for an extended time as the fighting of the civil war was getting steadily closer. That situation was made worse in that Louise was pregnant and needed to get back to the United States to give birth in a safer environment. After their departure from Biula, the threat was continuing to come daily closer so that George and Ena Wiseman too had to leave. Ruth took a vehicle and retreated to Luena where there appeared to be a little more security and an airport. Even there it soon became apparent that the UNITA opposition movement was closing in, so Ruth pleaded with the military to make room for both her and a vehicle on a military plane to Luanda, the capital. All was agreed with a military official. To her total incomprehension and consternation when it came to it, the military refused to listen to all her urgent pleading and refused to put either her or the vehicle on the plane. Imagine how she felt. She admitted honestly that she wept in despair wondering if God had also abandoned her to her inevitable fate.

The next day the news broke that the plane had crashed and all on board were killed. The Lord had graciously spared her life. She again approached the military who not only agreed but fulfilled their promise by taking both her and her vehicle safely to Luanda. She knew only too well that to be in the huge city of Luanda without a vehicle would be exceedingly difficult as there was no effective public transport.

Also, while she was living and working hard for the Lord in Luanda, she concentrated on working among the Chokwe people as she spoke Chokwe. On one occasion several of the elders who had come to Luanda from Saurimo had a conversation with her that touched her deeply. They posed her a question that had no easy answer. They wondered why the God of the Roman Catholic priests and nuns in Saurimo was so different from the God of the Protestant missionaries like the Wisemans and indeed herself. When she asked them to clarify why they said such a thing their reply shocked and upset her deeply. It was simply that when the situation in Saurimo got difficult and dangerous, the Roman Catholic missionaries didn't leave, they stayed on to encourage and help the people whereas the Protestant missionaries fled to safety. So, they concluded that they must be serving quite different gods. That hurt.

To be fair, they were not taking into account that all the missionaries at Biula, the Wisemans, Doris Pitman and Marjorie Beckwith were all much more elderly whereas most of the RC nuns and priests were very much younger, fitter and healthier and so more able to rough it. Additionally, their RC mission base was relatively safe within the city with good supplies available, whereas Biula was remote and exposed with not even a large village nearby never mind any supplies. Still, none of these factors seemed to be taken into consideration by these elders.

After much soul-searching and prayer, as soon as it was viable, Ruth made the remarkable decision to return to work and live within Saurimo not to Biula Mission Station. Mixed with her much patience and quiet determination the Lord eventually in His grace made it possible for her to find a privately-owned house which the Portuguese lady wanted to sell so that she could join her daughter in Portugal. There Ruth lived until just before the Lord took her home to glory in 2017. She remained through all the civil war when Saurimo was under attack and life became exceedingly difficult and personally dangerous. She shared in the often dire situation in that city under virtual siege with shortages of all kinds, including food and water. She too worked with candles for light and water off the roof stored in basins and the bath. In those bleak wartime days, both the water and electricity supply failed. At the same time, she kept on sharing as generously as possible and especially with the elderly and widows. She too got sick and had malaria with no access to a clinic or hospital worth the name. Indeed, at times she did her best to supply drugs to those in the hospital when otherwise none were available. She faithfully continued to explain and quietly comfort the believers with the words of Scripture that meant so much to her. God was utterly faithful even during all the horrors and sufferings of a relentless civil war. So too was His immense grace. Godly love was lived out in a thousand practical ways.

It will come as no surprise then when I say that she deservedly won the profound respect of believers and unbelievers, of government officials and all her neighbours. She helped so many in so many ways and the Lord faithfully supplied her needs. Often, she was satisfied with what most would consider totally inadequate basic needs. She won the hearts of her much-loved Chokwe people, who, may I add, are not always the easiest to love. They are often known as the 'cheeky Chokwe' but once their trust is won, they will be exceedingly loyal and will (almost) die for you, if necessary.

With that said, it will come as no great surprise when I say that Ruth was not easily frightened. One Christmas we decided to join her in Saurimo. We managed to get seats on a UN flight and take some goodies with us. Luggage was limited strictly to one small case and light hand luggage. So, it was an acquired art to carry a heavy turkey and trimmings to make it look quite light and certainly less than the required limit. We sometimes wondered why we didn't have a dislocated shoulder.

During the night sleep was suddenly disrupted by a series of heavy booms. Artillery fire. It didn't take long before some of the Christian young men came to reassure Donna Ruth. A mortar shell had landed in a road not far from the house but had done no serious harm. They usefully informed us that there would likely be only two more. We waited. Sure enough, another two mortar shells fell and then silence. The lads matter-of-factly explained that UNITA were capable of firing shells from out of town but couldn't stay long enough to fire more than three without their position being located. They could only fire off three rounds and then run. Wisdom gained from past experience. So we settled down to sleep the rest of the night.

We had a wonderful Christmas filled with good food, lots of fun, lots of laughs and precious times around the Word. But before Christmas Margaret and I spent days filling plastic sacks with a variety of goodies including precious items of food that were way beyond the ability of most to obtain. It is hard to forget the wizened, deeply wrinkled sad faces of elderly widows that were transformed into amazing smiles when they received their Christmas fare that included such basic things as cooking oil, sugar and salt as well as clothes and footwear. A visit to a war-torn African country reveals a level of abject poverty unheard of in the UK.

Kuito in the Province of Bié.

An area more difficult for us to access was the town of Kuito Bié on the south-central plateau, inland from Benguela which was an important port and the seaboard start of the former Benguela railway that previously linked Luena to the coast over 400 miles/650 klms away. Driving was completely out of the question. The railway lines and road bridges had been destroyed in the early years of the war as that area was hotly contested. The Umbundu tribe of Bie and Huambo were reported to predominantly support UNITA under their leader Jonas Savimbi. The whole struggle formed part of the long-range Cold War tussle between Russia and the USA. We were told by believers who knew him that Jonas Savimbi's father was a respected member of an assembly of believers. Sadly, sons don't always follow the good example of even a godly father.

In those early days, the railway had facilitated a series of evangelical mission stations with roots going back to David Livingstone and Fred Stanley Arnot. Livingstone had the ambitious objective of seeing a chain of evangelical Christian mission stations across much of central Africa from coast to coast. It had been a fertile area both for agriculture and the gospel with thriving mission station hospitals and schools that slowly but surely impacted the area, producing a new generation of better-educated men and women. So, it was more advanced than areas farther to the northeast that relentlessly opposed foreign attempts at building schools to educate a new generation. I recall how George Wiseman at Biula Mission Station told how local Chokwes on several occasions smashed the school desks he had laboriously made and refused to send their children to school. They even asked him to pay the children for attending school. Not so the Umbundu tribe.

So, it wasn't for nothing that the Umbundu tribe was part of a much larger area open to the gospel. It became known as part of 'The Beloved Strip' that also included large parts of modern-day Zambia – formerly N. Rhodesia - and Congo.

It was a privilege to respond to an invitation to spend some time in the town of Kuito in Bié province. We chose to go to encourage the believers shortly after a period of severe fighting had died down. Where could we stay? A local couple offered to put us up. That in itself was an education. They lived in what had been a well-built bungalow formerly owned by Charlie Shorten who had worked for many years on a relatively nearby mission station at Monte Esperança. As war approached, he bought a house in Kuito to act as a new base recognizing both the vulnerability and the desirability of mission stations to fighting forces both government and opposition. The many mission station buildings facilitated their camping needs as a military base in the bush. That purchase by Charlie Shorten was a surprising act of faith when others were keen to leave.

When we arrived at the airport just a few miles outside the town we were warmly welcomed by an excited small group of believers in a pickup truck. We rode in cramped style into the town, passing effortlessly through many roadblocks, our passage made easy by the presence of our accompanying believers who were well known and well respected by both police and army. We were informed that the pickup was borrowed temporarily from the local governor and was one of only three functioning vehicles remaining in the whole sizeable town. There were indeed plenty of other vehicles to be seen but we noticed that all were severely damaged by the fighting, riddled with bullet holes or cannibalised to try to keep other vehicles running.

The house where we stayed had a feature of unusual interest. During fighting a shell had exploded as it hit the roof, lifting the whole roof and allowing it to resettle, but about 2 inches/5 cms off the square. It still seemed to be quite stable. The large hole in the roof had been repaired as best they could with plastic sheeting and some tiles - no doubt rescued from another damaged building.

One bedroom had been retained as a room for visitors and contained the original furniture mostly unscathed including the original bed. The mattress had had to be refilled and in the absence of any other readily available suitable material was packed with corn husks. Somehow it had a large hollow in the middle. All our attempts at reshuffling the mattress stuffing didn't seem to work. We found it a bit of a challenge to find a comfortable spot conducive to sleep.

Outside there was a good-sized yard that was soon nicely filled with a group of men, some of whom had walked for days to hear the Bible teaching. It was noticeable that their clothes had seen better days and one man wore knee-high white wellington boots. Slowly but surely they told some – a very little bit - of their story. They had determined to come to hear the Bible teaching but when they approached the outskirts of Kuito they realised that their clothes were in such rags that they were indecent by town standards, so they sent a young lad into the town to contact the elders and ask for clothes. Years of war had brought them all to near destitution. The word went out and the believers from their scarcity sacrificed what they could to send adequate clothing to their brothers in Christ. These were some of the men we had come to encourage in the Lord. The style and colour of their clothes were the least of their concerns.

They listened with excellent attention as I opened God's Word. After listening to me teaching I was deeply humbled when an elderly man said in Portuguese something like 'I see your face, but I hear the voice of Ernest Wilson'. [His grandson is a missionary in Waterford, S. Ireland and a gifted Bible teacher.] I have never had a richer compliment about my teaching of the Word. T.E.Wilson was a spiritual giant who, with his wife Elizabeth, had worked for many years among the Songo and Umbundu tribes and had seen a tremendous work done for the Lord, not only in preaching but also in consistent systematic rich Bible teaching. We heard him teach in N. Ireland when we were young. Like Moses, his face seemed to shine with the presence of the Lord and his teaching was always Christ-exalting. We met him once in Angola at the airport in Saurimo as he prepared to fly out at the end of his final visit to Angola whereas we were on our first visit.

I shall never forget the experience of standing outside that house in Kuito hearing the muffled sound of hundreds of people walking quietly in the streets, mostly down the middle for there were no vehicles circulating. Many had bare feet, the rest with the simplest of flip-flops. It was an eerie unforgettable sound, the sound of determined daily courage going to cultivate and trade enough to survive. The so-called Lord's Prayer (really the Disciples' Prayer) was very relevant for these people – 'Give us this day our bread, enough for today'.

An equally vivid memory was the sound of passing troops out for their early morning fitness run, singing rhythmically and enthusiastically as only Africans can do. Many might soon lose their lives, but they could sing as if they hadn't a care in the world.

Walking everywhere was another unforgettable experience. If we dared to look up as we passed close to buildings shattered by rockets, roofs gone, walls pock-marked by bullets and heavy artillery damage, there were chunks of masonry over-hanging the footpaths, held in place by the slimmest of metal reinforcing rods. Was it safe? Probably not.

On our first visit the large hall had a roof but not much by way of side walls. Bricks and blocks were both scarce and expensive and where could sand and cement be found? Later, with the generous financial help of a long retired American missionary, Don Cole, they built a lovely larger hall on the same site. It seated about 1,000 – African style. They do not have the westerners' insistence on personal space. We noticed that when a long bench looked like it was already full, another woman would squeeze in. There would be a few wiggles and she was seated. The same would happen several times more. With temperatures in excess of 25⁰ C it makes for warm fellowship. To be fair, the elders would always ensure that Margaret had a suitably spaced chair while I would be respectfully seated on or near the platform.

We visited several times for two weeks over Easter. I would teach each afternoon for several hours by interpretation. Many of the older women spoke little or no Portuguese. One of the things that amazed me was the number of younger women who came in good time so as to occupy the front rows of seats. Men on one side, women on the other. They came with notebooks (often school exercise books). I quickly discovered that many of the young men had missed most if not all of their secondary schooling as they were obliged to stay hidden in the bush to avoid being forcibly conscripted at gunpoint into either of the two sides of the conflict. Education was secondary to the need to stay alive by avoiding participating in a war many of them did not want. Tragically it was quite possible to have brothers from the same family on opposing sides of the fighting. Is it any wonder that sometimes their aim was none too accurate? We were shown where the dividing line had run down the middle of a wide street. Civil war is a merciless ugly thing.

As we listened to stories of the recent fighting, three stand out in my memory.

When the fighting had been fierce in the part of town where the house where we were staying was located and shelling was frequent, the family made a tough choice. The garage at the side of the house had a strong thick concrete floor, so they burrowed underneath it by digging out as best they could sufficient space for little more than a double bed mattress. For many months that was where they spent their nights and sometimes their days as well. Near a wall at the side of the house was a peach tree that had never given any fruit but that year it gave an abundant crop that just kept on coming. For many months that is what kept the family alive. The tree was still there when we visited but had never again given fruit. Moreover, they managed to punch a hole in the wall and pass peaches to their neighbours to help them stay alive as well. That neighbouring family were not believers, but you can understand that they were deeply grateful.

Does it surprise anyone that they saw in that peach tree the near miraculous provision of a loving heavenly Father? Only God could do that. How it strengthened their severely tested faith.

As I write during the Covid 19 lockdown, people are complaining strongly about an intolerable level of stress and isolation, talking about 'internet poverty' for school-age children and the government's responsibility to feed children during school holidays. I sometimes wonder how our modern society would cope with the whole family – parents and four children - staying underground in darkness for more than six months with little more than some rainwater to drink and peaches to eat. How important would 'internet poverty' appear?

A second memory is impossible to erase. On one occasion the grandfather of the family became so desperate that his grandchildren were exceedingly short of nourishment that he ventured out hoping to find some food for sale. He had barely walked 10 metres when a sniper's bullet killed him on the spot. His body lay there until after dark when some of the family risked their own life to drag the body back to the house. He was buried in the small patch of garden. So, as we walked along the same road, we were amazed to see a mound of earth and sometimes several in almost every front garden. Unforgettable memories.

Years later the government undertook the gruesome task of exhuming all the bodies and reburying them in the proper cemetery.

A third very different but powerful memory remains vivid. Even when the worst of the fighting passed it was still unwise for the believers to risk meeting in their halls or church buildings so they decided that believers who lived near each other would meet before dawn each morning in someone's home. A passage of Scripture would be read before a time of earnest prayer, ending while it was still dark so that everyone could slip out quietly unseen. They were still doing that when we were there the first time. About ten of us met to pray. For us, sometimes we couldn't even make out who people were but some we recognised by their voices, just shadowy figures that lovingly grasped our hands. Prayer was real and from the heart as they prayed to the Lord for one another and for unsaved relatives to come to Christ. Life was very uncertain for all. There was but a step between everyone and death.

So, these many small groups of praying believers clung to the Lord and to each other. Many came out of that lockdown stronger in their faith and with a devotion to the Lord and to each other that was wonderful to witness.

On the brighter side, there was a time when the UK government were getting rid of some World War 2 wartime emergency supplies. Hammer mills combined with an appropriate diesel generator were being disposed of. Medical Missionary News obtained several and one was offered to us in Angola. It was brutishly big and heavy but in good working condition. After it had sat in one of our many containers for more than a year while the war raged in the provinces, an improvement in the situation came. Kuito, an excellent maize-growing area, was the ideal location to make the best use of a maize mill. The United Nations were approached and imagine our delight when they undertook to transport it to Kuito to help relieve the food shortage.

The Kuito elders organized a group of men capable of running it and they did a marvellous job with integrity. They charged a low fee per kilo but still at the end of every day, the leftover grain was carefully brushed up and a regular allowance was given free of charge to a list of needy widows. The mill was a great blessing.

On more than one occasion we made the effort to arrive in Kuito more than a week before Easter. Remember there were no scheduled flights. On the afternoons I taught the events of each day in the week before the Lord's crucifixion, often referred to as Passion Week. The interest was most encouraging as we built up to the trial and crucifixion of the Lord. Numbers attending increased steadily until several hundred were attending each Bible-teaching session. A large blackboard was pressed into service. It worked well as I filled it with essential notes in Portuguese each day before the teaching session began. Of course, some discovered what I was doing and simply came earlier to have the time to write down their notes and then listen to the teaching. It was wonderful to see such enthusiasm to hear the teaching of God's divinely inspired word, remembering that everyone had to walk and some from quite a long distance. I do not recall seeing any bicycles. It was quite moving as the believers were enthralled again by the inexplicable incomprehensible love of the Lord that took Him through the Upper Room, betrayal, His utterly unjust trial, Gethsemane and then to Calvary. They waited in joyful anticipation of the resurrection story. We sensed the presence of the Lord in a special way.

It was wonderful to have the health to be able to walk everywhere like everyone else. It was surprisingly relaxing as well as healthy to walk through clear air in a town with so few vehicles causing any pollution.

Before we arrived on our first visit it seemed that word got out somehow that we were involved in procuring the hammer maize mill. On Easter Sunday I was invited to preach the gospel in the largest hall in Kuito. Not only was it full with about 1,000 people, as estimated by the elders, but another 500 or so were sheltered from the sun and seated outside under a selection of tarpaulins. A large team of volunteers had worked very hard to have everything in order.

I recall preaching on Romans 1:16 - *'For I am not ashamed of the gospel of Christ for it is the power of God for salvation to everyone who believes'* - and those right with God will go on making decisions that reflect their faith. It was impossible not to delight in the story of the resurrection. The message was translated into Umbundu by one of the elders, Bernardo Capeio, a godly man with a true shepherd heart. It was interesting, as at times he would speak quietly to me saying in Portuguese to the effect – 'now just hold on a minute'. He would then amplify the point I was making and drive it home with passion in Umbundu before he would give me the signal to continue. We worked well as a team. He was a precious brother whom we respected highly and was dearly loved by his people, a real biblical pastor-elder.

There was rapt attention and the clear perception that the Holy Spirit was speaking. At the end I asked all those sincerely wanting to know how they could trust Christ as their Saviour, not to leave but to sit in their seat and then move to the front seats. More than ten remained to talk with the elders as arranged previously with them. One woman was clearly quite agitated. As an elder tried to point her to Christ, she had what appeared to me a peculiar reaction. What followed showed the wisdom of that elder and so different from what I was inclined to do.

She asked permission to go home and come back a little later in the afternoon. She had quite some way to walk. My inclination was to say – no, it must be settled now. Little did I know. The elder said that it was OK and he would wait until she returned. I thought that was maybe a bit foolish as she probably wouldn't return at all. So we waited and waited and waited. I decided to stay with the group of elders as we prayed for the genuine repentance and salvation of souls and for this woman in particular.

She returned and to my amazement was carrying a large basket which she set down on the ground in front of us as we stood in the open space in front of the building. That basket had a host of weird and wonderful items, some of which I had seen before but many I had never seen previously. They were all part of her witchcraft paraphernalia. She was well known to the elders and to the large crowd that had gathered outside - a highly feared witch who had a real evil devilish influence in the community.

She said that she was now ready to trust Christ and abandon witchcraft. Then she simply asked the elders to burn the whole basketful of fetishes. The crowd was growing larger. I shall never forget what the elders said. They firmly refused and I began to think 'maybe they too are scared' but then they quickly added words to the effect 'No, *you* must burn the lot' and to my further amazement reached her a bundle of dried grass and a match. She took the bundle of grass and set the lot on fire. What a significant bonfire. The crowd were silent.

Then one of the elders said simply 'Now are you ready to trust Christ?' and there and then explained the gospel to her yet again and led her to faith in Christ alone. Her public confession of faith in Christ as her Saviour and Lord was electrifying to the onlooking crowd. Presumably, at least some of that crowd from the nearby market had 'consulted' her and paid her well for her services. To whom would they go now? Was she really changed or was this just a show? And how would she support herself financially? In Ephesus the silversmiths were bitterly opposed to the impact of the gospel on their business opportunities.

During the week after Easter Sunday, it was decided that we should go to the village of Cunji about three or four kilometres outside of Kuito where there were some from several small assemblies who could all meet in the hall in Cunji. It would facilitate believers who had no access to transport and though some had walked to Kuito and back most of the older folks could not manage it as the road went down into a valley and then back up quite a long steep hill. Those were precious days in Cunji though with much smaller numbers than in Kuito.

I always thought that such spiritual victories in Kuito had much less to do with the preacher than the fervent prayers of so many believers who had met morning by morning before dawn to pray for a work of the Lord in hearts and minds in their beloved town. It was lovely to see how they were encouraged in their faith in the Lord as they enjoyed the study of His Word simply explained and also saw people trust Christ.

There were assemblies outside of Kuito and some at quite some distance away. Reaching them was not only difficult because of the lack of vehicles but also because throughout that whole area explosive landmines had been laid on roads as well as around water holes and on village paths. Women and children were often maimed or killed as they went to fetch water.

The suggestion was made that we could spend a Sunday with the believers at an outlying assembly at Kunninga as the road there was reportedly recently declared free of landmines. The United Nations had a specialised de-mining team based in Kuito. They were systematically but painfully slowly locating and removing landmines from the rural dirt roads. Many de-miners lost their life. Some will remember the carefully staged fund-raising photograph of Princess Diana in Angola detonating landmines.

When we went to check with the de-miners, it was interesting to discover an Irish man who had left the RC priesthood, joined the British army and then became the head of a de-mining team. A colourful fascinating man. He was most helpful when we explained our mission and our intended destination. He explained that at the side of the road they carefully placed white stones indicating that the de-miners had cleared the road. On no account should we even step beyond these stones at the side never mind risk turning the Landrover by going even a few centimetres beyond these stones.

He agreed that we would call with him again on Sunday morning before we left. They would send out a special team to re-check the road as it was not unknown for mines to be placed again on the road after it had been de-mined the previous day. Evidently, there were still nearby those unhappy with the de-mining process.

After the morning visit, we were given the all-clear. It was with due care that we drove ensuring that we spotted the white stones and stayed well within the demarcations.

What a reception we received as several hundred sang and danced their welcome just so genuinely glad not only that we visited them but that they were reunited with some brothers from Kuito whom they had not seen for a long time. Life had become so precarious, risky and uncertain. Good friends were never sure when or if they would see each other again in this life.

The Breaking of Bread was simple but very moving. It seemed to us that many were just so glad that their lives had been spared to allow them and us to remember the Lord another time. That Christ had loved us so much that He voluntarily had given His life to save us from eternal death was – and indeed is – an amazing truth that still touches hearts and evokes worship.

That journey was the first time we had seen so many metal signs on short poles on both sides of the road on which were painted a skull and crossed bones with the message 'Perigo - Minas' (Danger-Landmines).

Visits to provincial capital towns, whether Luena, Saurimo or Kuito were encouraging to the believers who were enthusiastically welcoming and kind to us, even when their material circumstances were a daily struggle. It was humbling that they so generously shared from their meagre supplies. It was also an encouragement to us to see so many groups of believers meeting regularly and reaching out with the gospel, seeing people profess faith, being baptised and very simply remembering the Lord each Lord's Day. Looking back, yes it was tiring and hard work. The amazing thing was how the Lord graciously preserved us in good health with no serious problems despite living in some very basic accommodation though of course, we took all reasonable precautions.

Some amazing weaknesses also became apparent. We cannot forget one rural Chokwe assembly where there was no one who could read, so each Lord's Day they invited someone from the village, often a young man who could read, to come and read passages of Scripture to them. That person was frequently not a believer. How was it possible for them to function as a local church? How could there be 'elders' able to teach who couldn't read? Full marks for persistence. The low educational level in some villages meant that too many men could neither read nor write.

Benguela and Lobito

There was a stage in the ongoing civil war when the government managed to make reasonably secure the coast road from Luanda leading south to Benguela which used to be the coastal end of the great Benguela railway system built to open up the interior of Angola and indeed far beyond. It was an amazing feat of engineering but was destroyed in the war. Many bridges were blown up deliberately while others were cannibalised and the metal sleepers used for house building and fencing in a desperate society where at times just about everything, including the basics, were in very short supply or simply not available at all.

So it was that in 1996 in discussion with brother Cabita in the Cuca assembly that we attended, he agreed to accompany us down the coastal road to Benguela and Lobito where we were told there were quite a few assemblies and we had met some believers from there who had attended a conference in Luanda. It would be our first trip to that area and would be about 1,500 klms.

To our surprise, despite having sent word in advance to allow for various meetings to be arranged, when we arrived in Lobito, it was to discover that nothing had been arranged in advance, so we just had to make the best use of the existing weekly timetable of meetings. There was a feeling of crosscurrents whether personality clashes or whatever but we detected two quite different reactions. For some they expressed their deep appreciation with pleas to return to teach the Word of God. At the same time on the part of their leadership there was a distinct coolness and perceived disinterest in the teaching of Scripture. It soon became apparent that some men had managed to get themselves into positions of influence in some of the larger assemblies who were keen to be seen as 'pastors' but were not willing or incapable of truly caring for and feeding the sheep. We were struck by the lack of basic understanding of the Scriptures and sadly what passed for Bible teaching. Just about everywhere we went there was a plea from many ordinary believers to return and teach the Word of God. It was rather like the Lord when he had compassion on the people for they were like sheep without a shepherd.

That visit was remarkable for another reason in that on the Sunday, the day before our planned return to Luanda on Monday it rained heavily and incessantly. Word filtered through from travellers coming from Luanda that a bridge was in bad shape and that there would be a risk that it would not survive. That route was of course the only road link from Benguela north to Luanda. What made it worse was that we had made an airline booking to leave Luanda on the Wednesday.

As we travelled north from Benguela we rapidly became aware of the almost total absence of traffic heading south. A few vehicles may have joined from farms. As we approached the bridge there was a long queue of vehicles parked on the roadside. Some were prepared for a long stay as they were cooking meals beside their trucks. A brief chat with bystanders confirmed that the bridge was down. When we reached where the bridge had been we were informed that the torrent of water had piled up broken trees, damming the water until the bridge could withstand no more. It was gone.

A chat with the many spectators revealed that only two vehicles had succeeded in crossing by descending a steep muddy slope, making their way through the river and then climbing up an equally steep bank on the other side. A glance down the steep slope on our side revealed a collection of abandoned vehicles. Of the two vehicles one was a large American 4x4. Happily, the other was a Landrover Defender like ours.

In Angola every disaster brings an opportunity. A bunch of young lads assured me that we could make it OK and that they would push us if we should stick – for a small fee. In jest I made them a counteroffer. If I needed them, I would pay, but if I didn't need them then they would pay me. That caused a major heated discussion as to the probabilities. Of course, they were penniless.

I walked down the slope, walked through the water and up the far side. The water had receded enough to be waded by a Landrover and the riverbed was lovely firm sand. Low gear ratio and four wheel drive allowed us to descend safely, ford the river and with some scrabbling reach the road on the other side to the cheers of the crowd. We needed no assistance. It was our joy to pay the would be 'helpers' and also give them Christian reading material and a gospel calendar. Yes, every disaster brings an opportunity.

Again, we thanked the Lord for safe travel and prayed that both our teaching of the Scriptures and literature distributed in various locations would bear fruit.

Chapter 8
TIME TO LEAVE ANGOLA

There is no doubt that over 13 years visits to the rural provinces but especially the stresses of Luanda city life took their toll on us physically, mentally and emotionally. As those stresses just kept on increasing it soon became obvious that our time in Luanda was coming towards a close.

Several indicators were pointing in the same direction. First were health problems. On several occasions I simply dropped. I recall one such episode as we left our flat and were walking along the corridor leading to the staircase. I threw my arms round a concrete pillar as I sunk to the floor. Margaret was just behind me. That was not the only time it happened and what made it worse was that it was without any apparent warning. I began to wonder what would happen if I had a repeat episode while driving. Clearly, I was going to need medical attention not available locally.

A Christian friend and fellow missionary from Switzerland brought a portable ECG machine to our flat. His advice was abundantly clear and unequivocal. We must head back to the UK without delay for me to have more detailed medical examination. He also insisted that we needed time away from the very high stress levels of life in Luanda. He knew all about living in Luanda.

A second factor also came into play. With the arrival of peace, many of the internally displaced people were making preparations to return to their places of origin from which they had fled but still regarded as home. That meant that men who had been attending the study classes were no longer available. That phase of the work was clearly coming to an end. We had spent thirteen very busy and fruitful years preaching and teaching but they were coming to an end.

Special farewell events were arranged, including the Cuca Portuguese-speaking assembly where we had enjoyed warm fellowship on Lord's Days for quite a few years among predominantly Umbundu believers and for whom we had developed a real respect and love. They presented us with a lovely plaque expressing their deep appreciation for all the help we had given in their assembly and to their many friends in other assemblies.

And so it was that we said many emotional farewells to those whom we had grown to love and respect and departed from Luanda airport back to Ballymena.

In many ways leaving a country and the work to which the Lord had called us, preserved us, protected us and to some small extent used us was much more traumatic than arriving there in the first place. Arriving carries with it all the excitement of starting out with the Lord's help and guidance to begin to fulfil a desire that the Lord had placed on our hearts. Leaving was with a mixture of thankfulness to the Lord and sorrow that we hadn't succeeded in doing much more, seeing more trust Christ and more really growing in their faith. Our fundamental guidelines had been 2 Timothy 2v2 and the three T's – teach, train and trust.

Of course, the history of missionary activity reveals that sometimes when the Lord permits circumstances that remove all the missionaries, the gospel really prospers in a way it never had previously. We could point to China with the arrival of the Communist regime and the forced expulsion of several hundred evangelical missionaries; likewise Ethiopia as outlined in Robert Revie's book 'India to Ethiopia'. And what shall we say about Iran and some other Muslim countries where the spiritual bankruptcy of unfettered Islam becomes apparent even to nominally faithful followers? Absolute power corrupts absolutely in both secular and supposedly religious regimes. Sinful human nature needs a much deeper remedy than unthinking religious observance.

Chapter 9
MOVING TO ZAMBIA

When it became clear to us that our thirteen-year period of service to the Lord based in the capital city of Luanda in Angola had come to an end, we returned to Ballymena. After a time of rest and recovery, much prayer and careful consultation, we concluded that it should be possible to continue to serve the Lord in a less stressful location than Luanda.

Our minds turned to the many open doors and opportunities we had seen in Zambia and indeed the very warm welcome that had been accorded us. As we looked back to our earlier visit, in many ways it seemed relatively easy to consider seeking to serve the Lord in Zambia where there seemed to be both great need and an open door. Once again we shared our thinking with our elders and many of our friends as we all together prayerfully sought the Lord's will and direction for us. It confirmed our own thinking as all were unanimous in concluding that the Lord was indeed behind this desire. It was so reassuring that we were being guided by the Lord. But in which town should we stay and how would we find a house?

Our stay in Zambia was made amazingly easy in that the Lord wonderfully provided us with both a house and a vehicle. Alan and Sheila Park were back on furlough in Scotland, their home country, but as soon as they heard of our interest in going to Zambia they very graciously offered to loan us their fully equipped house in Luanshya and their

Isuzu vehicle. What an unexpected answer to prayer that was. That enabled us to visit other locations on the Copperbelt including Ndola, Chingola and Kitwe. It became evident that Kitwe was a strategically central town for the whole of the Copperbelt and we felt drawn to explore where and how we could serve the Lord there.

But while living in Luanshya we quickly got a glimpse of what the Emmaus Bible Correspondence work involved, including meeting the believers who regularly took courses to outlying areas to facilitate a much wider distribution. They had been accustomed to come together regularly for Bible Study and prayer time with Alan and Sheila and wondered if we would hold Bible Studies with them. It was a joy to do so.

What was more, those same believers were keen that we should visit the various assemblies from which they came so that door was also wide open even though we didn't speak Bemba. They always arranged for someone to translate for me.

Through another fascinating sequence of events, the elders from one Zambian assembly in Kitwe invited us to join them at a meeting where they would be hearing reports from those leading various aspects of the assembly's work and praying together as to how the work could be advanced. That gave us a revealing overall insight into what was already happening but what made quite an impression on us was the warmness of their welcome as they made abundantly clear that they would be happy for us to attend that assembly if the Lord so directed our steps.

Finding a house to rent in Kitwe was not a simple matter in that there were no estate agents in those days. The few houses that we managed to find were far from suitable. Eventually one of the elders and his wife, Dr Henry and Mrs Rose Mugala suggested that we take a look at some houses in a secluded safe complex with about thirty houses surrounded by a high wall topped with an electric fence. It had only one entrance with security guards day and night. We looked at spacious bungalows in total disbelief that we could ever afford such rents. Inquiries revealed that one would become available soon, but we would have to apply and have an interview with the controlling board. The rent quoted was acceptable, but would we pass the board's requirements and scrutiny? It was quite reassuring that when we explained our purpose in locating to Kitwe several of the board members were immediately sympathetic. We had wondered how they would react as they generally only rented to those with guaranteed salaries in firms related to the big mining companies. How would they consider people with no salary or guaranteed income? To our relief they accepted our request and shortly afterwards we completed the necessary legal formalities. We remained there for the following thirteen years. The Lord arranged for us just the house we needed and where we needed to be.

It was so evidently the Lord's provision of a safe secure location especially when Margaret was frequently on her own while I was busy away teaching and preaching sometimes quite a distance from home.

One of the totally unexpected advantages of that house in a secluded complex was that it wasn't too difficult to try to get to know at least some of our neighbours. Some were only short termers but others stayed in the same house for several years. It was a new experience for us to have so many Indian neighbours and some years after we settled there, it was such a joy to discover that one Indian couple were lovely believers who were only too happy to have a Bible Study and time of fellowship regularly in their house. Not only so but they invited many Indian friends to their home for special events to commemorate and explain the meaning of Christmas and

Easter. It was a privilege to try to help them understand the significance and meaning of these biblical events and their relevance to our faith and daily lives.

We were always most impressed with how polite and respectful these dear Indian friends were as we explained the historical facts and the Bible record that were the basis for a real and meaningful salvation from the consequences and power of sin in our lives.

Lesson 1
College Bible Studies

But what exactly did the Lord have in mind for us to do in Kitwe? We prayed and expected the Lord to guide us.

One Sunday afternoon soon after we moved into our new accommodation a young man named Morris Lupanda approached me and asked us if we could help him. He was struggling to take a weekly Bible Study in a secondary school teacher-training college some half an hour's drive outside of Kitwe. Could we help? Permission from the college authorities had already been obtained. So we gave him a lift as he had no car and had to depend on minibuses or taxi's. It was a totally unexpected joy to take him weekly to study the Scriptures in a college, something we had longed to do in Angola but it was never allowed by the communist authorities. He was delighted when we offered to continue to help with these Bible studies with 18-20 students. After that first study, he then mentioned that there was another weekly Bible study, this time in the local School of Nursing attached to the large Kitwe regional hospital. It was only ten minutes from our house. There too help was needed.

When we first met Morris he was single and quite discouraged as he was unemployed. We encouraged him as best we could to get some training. He wanted to be an electrician. What a joy it was when the Lord answered prayer and after some time he not only qualified but got a job in the copper mines as a qualified electrician. But another joy was also in store for him. Totally unknown to me he was attracted to a young lady in one of those early Bible Studies. She was studying to be a maths teacher and still had two years to go. It says something about the calibre of the young man that he refrained from making his feelings known until she qualified. He explained that he didn't want her to be distracted from her studies and if it was the Lord's will, they both would wait. Needless to say, it was with great pleasure that Margaret and I attended their wedding and as the years passed rejoiced with them at the birth of their children.

Amazing as it seemed to us, we had never before conducted Bible studies in colleges or universities, but the Lord amazingly opened the door and we were delighted to help. Could we cope? What a joy it was to study the Scriptures with college students in Kitwe with the added bonus that it could all be in English, the language of secondary and college education.

Once we became better known we also received requests to help with Bible studies in another three locations, one of them like a technical college, another a college training primary school teachers and occasionally yet another based in a believer's home with up to forty university undergraduates. It was heartening to see that this last group already had capable leadership so my visits were only to encourage them.

Though Margaret had no pretensions to be a great guitar player, it was a wonderful help as we taught new hymns and choruses that the students thoroughly enjoyed and would take with them wherever their career would take them. For that reason we compiled and photocopied a good selection of the newer choruses we taught them so that each student had a copy.

On one occasion at that very first college we visited, we asked how they managed to attend any local church on Sundays as the college was well out of Kitwe and up a long lane. In fact, it was so remote that we occasionally spotted monkeys swinging between the trees and crossing the earth track. It soon became obvious that to attend almost any local church it was quite a long walk to reach the tarmac road and then also expensive on the irregular Sunday local minibuses. Like many students, many of them were already battling to pay their college fees. It was obvious that we should help.

Wooden bench seats were made for the back of our Toyota pickup. We were glad that we had ordered a fibreglass canopy which would cope with the wet season. It was a case of girls inside the twin cab pickup – as many as could squeeze in - and the lads on the wooden benches in the back, but there never was a complaint. So began a long Sunday morning tradition of collecting a load of students to attend our assembly where they would hear the Word of God expounded and the way of salvation made plain. Some who were baptised believers thoroughly enjoyed the Breaking of Bread.

For most of the earlier years we were there, it was good that the traffic police didn't normally work on a Sunday when movement was normally lighter and indeed there were fewer cars on the road. If truth be told, we often were overloaded by European standards as we squashed in all who wanted to attend. And could the students sing. In Zambia journeys are for singing – either in English or more commonly in Bemba which most spoke as their mother tongue.

So it was that the Lord wonderfully opened totally unexpected doors. It was His doing that we had the opportunity to teach His Word to students, answering the many questions, clarifying what salvation is and is not and sometimes as graciously as possible confronting unbiblical ideas from a variety of denominational churches. Young people with some knowledge of Scripture the world over want to know how they can discern the Lord's will and especially who they should marry. They wanted to know what is involved in setting up a Christian home. What does the Bible teach about sex – including before marriage? Do Christians have to keep the Old Testament Law? does the Bible teach that a real believer should never be sick, should always succeed financially and will always have all their prayers answered as they would like? From their future earnings, how much money should be given to God and His work? Can a Christian be saved and then later lose their salvation? What does repentance mean? The list goes on and on. Yes, it truly was a wonderful privilege and a joy to dig more deeply into Scripture to find the highly relevant answers to such pressing questions.

So, among many other topics, we studied the whole of John's Gospel together. To unbelievers, the need for salvation by faith in the finished work of Christ on the Cross was clearly evident. To some it came as quite a shock that all their church-attendance, good as it was, would not in any way earn their salvation.

John McQuoid's book 'Knowing and Doing' we found to be exceedingly useful. We studied it chapter by chapter and as we did so, we wrote a series of questions after each lesson. We divided the students into smaller groups to answer and discuss the questions then come together to summarize what had been learned. The beauty of John's excellent book was that it covered so many widely varied topics and gave an excellent base for some more extended additional studies when we saw that it was required. Those studies were used of the Lord and were a wonderful blessing to many. They had an additional blessing in that they were able to keep the photocopied notes. We provided every student with A4 files both to keep their college notes together and also to preserve their Bible Study notes for future reference and use. Only eternity will reveal the value of John McQuoid's patient careful orderly compilation of those studies. They were such a blessing.

It didn't take long to learn that in addition to John's excellent book, the students wanted copies of our notes in every college study, so there too everyone was provided with a detailed set of Bible teaching notes on a wide range of topics and some Bible books. Our hope was that as they compiled all these notes over their three or four years of college study, they would end up with material that they could re-study and re-teach wherever the Lord provided them with a teaching post or in the case of the nurses in a nursing clinic or hospital.

We are so thankful to the Lord that we have heard from 'our' students in parts of Zambia far from Kitwe who continue to use those notes. In at least one case, in Bible Studies in a teacher-training college.

As in Angola, we quickly recognised the need for Bibles and especially Study Bibles. 'There were no nearby bookshops selling Study Bibles or good Christian literature at affordable prices as in the UK. Ian and Marilyn Campbell had opened and stocked an excellent Bible bookshop in Chingola but that was a considerable distance away for most students based in and around Kitwe. That's where Opal Trust of Lockerbie proved of inestimable worth. Geoff and Janet Ruston together with John Lewis had set up Opal Trust to help those in less developed countries have access to Bibles and good Christian literature at much-reduced prices. The students couldn't possibly afford first-world prices. So it was that we imported by container many boxes of Bibles and especially Study Bibles with lots of helpful explanatory notes.

As one way to help further lower costs to students, we invented a scheme. Basically, a record was kept of weekly attendance and those who didn't miss once in ten weeks were entitled to choose one of the various Bibles and Study Bibles we had to offer for a minimal payment of the equivalent of about £2. That meant that the great majority of college students who attended these studies went away with a Study Bible. In fact, for those who evidently were struggling even to pay that amount, the price became a lower nominal sum. No one who 'earned' a Bible by their attendance ever left without receiving it.

I still remember the obvious enthusiasm with which a lovely nursing student came to her first study after receiving her Bible. She came with a beaming smile as she kept her finger in the place. She came directly to me and asked me if I knew what she had just learned. She was thrilled and excited at what she had discovered for herself in her Bible study. Imagine, young people were actually excited about reading their Bible and full of interesting questions as they dug deeper.

As some of the young men who accompanied me to these various studies always carried the boxes of Bibles and other literature to and from the pickup, they gave these boxes the humorous title of being 'heavy theology'.

It never ceased to make us thankful that the Lord motivated believers to support us financially so generously that we could afford to subsidise Bibles to hundreds of students and young people over the years. They will have their rightful reward from the Lord.

One of the things that amazed us was how polite all our Zambian college students were. 'Greeting' in Zambian culture is absolutely essential. Most students would quite naturally come and greet both Margaret and me before they would take their seats. Likewise, after the Bible study was finished, most would come and thank us as they said good-bye. They became our friends.

Another culturally accepted tradition took a little getting used to. That was seeing teenage lads on the streets, 'greeting' by shaking hands and holding hands quite naturally and affectionately without any of the undertones which we westerners would normally associate with men or teenage lads holding hands as they chatted on the street.

The college Bible Studies opened up yet another avenue in that each year when our local church fellowship held a week of outreach gospel meetings, we would set aside one evening specifically for college and university students. It needed and fully merited a special effort by several members to transport all who wanted to attend from the various colleges, but it was well worthwhile as they had an excellent opportunity to hear the gospel explained in all its wonderful simplicity and were invited to respond personally to the clear challenge of the message. Only the Lord can evaluate the results of those meetings and the genuineness of decisions made.

One such special time was not quickly forgotten by us as Sam Balmer from Enniskillen in N. Ireland was visiting Zambia and was able to free his schedule to speak each night during one of those special weeks.

From time to time we would invite a group of students to come to our house for a special evening of singing, prayer, Bible study and food. Margaret would have been busy in the kitchen making all sorts of culinary delights but in later years we sometimes simply bought pizzas or so-called 'junk food' – something which most of them could never afford but thoroughly enjoyed. They so much enjoyed trying out what they called 'English food' and indeed just seeing what our home was like. We quickly became 'Uncle Eric' and 'Auntie Margaret' to a large number of young people now scattered over Zambia. We can't forget how one University student admitted that he had never eaten ice cream before. He carefully tested just a very small portion first before deciding that it was good, indeed it was very good, and he could even cope with a second helping.

The Lord was giving us an incalculable privilege as He taught us slowly but surely how to share the eternal truths of His divinely inspired Word that would impact young lives for Christ.

Under the good guiding hand of God, another development fed very naturally into the student work. In our local assembly the members were divided into home groups according to the area where they lived. We happily joined one in our area. The home of the Chomba family in which we met had three boys and a fourth, a relation, living with them. As the years passed and they grew up, they not only came to faith in Christ but began to grow spiritually. So it was with great pleasure that we encouraged them to join us in the student ministry. From their first tentative steps they grew in competence and courage until one by one they were well able to lead the smaller sub-divided discussion groups and then the whole larger group. It was a story of patiently encouraging them to develop their God-given gifts and abilities.

A bonus was that two of them were gifted musically. Margaret used her guitar to accompany the singing in our home group. On one occasion she noticed one of the lads trying to strum her guitar, so began to teach him the basics and he learned quickly. When we were leaving for a furlough she asked him if he would take care of her guitar while she was away. By the time we returned he had been making rapid progress and never stopped improving when we guided him towards more proficient musicians.

So it was that the Lord was teaching us that as each young man developed, we should relish the joy of building them into the team that visited the colleges. They learned to lead both in the singing and in the Bible studies, but we were always there to support and encourage them. We were learning to work hard to move towards becoming redundant.

Looking back, we can see how the Lord was teaching us how vital was their contribution. For one thing, they were closer in age to the students and were full of youthful energy. They understood their own culture better than we could ever do. They could sing some choruses in Bemba that spoke to the heart. They understood the cultural negative pressures as well as the taboos when it came to trying to understand the sometimes deeply felt emotional conflict between their culture and God's infallible Word. Sheer youthful enthusiasm combined with musical ability made for a much more effective college team that in turn not only attracted more college students to attend but also helped to clarify the claims of Christ in a culturally sensitive way.

Before long we began to realise that we could keep adding in other young people, young men and young ladies, who could be mentored and encouraged in the safety of the small college student groups. Later, for several of them, the Lord began to use them in our local assembly which clearly was a much larger group. They had gained useful experience and increasing confidence in the smaller college Bible studies. It was a training ground for us and for them.

Lesson 2
Bible teaching outside of Kitwe

When the believers with whom we met to study God's Word in Luanshya heard that the Lord had opened the way for us to relocate to Kitwe, they made an interesting suggestion. One dear brother in particular, Mr Mwila, who was just about blind had been a dedicated evangelist and had seen people come to know the Lord but realised he no longer could help them with teaching and encouragement the way he formerly did. He asked if I would be willing to travel to Misaka, some kilometres outside of Luanshya, to teach the

the Masaiti Camp site many of them took up the opportunity. It was good for them in several respects for not only did they benefit from the teaching, but they thoroughly enjoyed both the tranquillity of a lovely rural setting in the middle of the bush near a stream, but they also linked up with young people from other surrounding assemblies. Young believers need the company of other young believers as was evidenced by the enjoyable times they had after the formal teaching sessions.

There was one matter about which I struggled to know if I had been unwise and had made a mistake. Soon after I started travelling to Misaka and Masaiti, there was a critical shortage of food because of a bad harvest. Many were hungry and it was easy to see that especially some of the older people were losing weight and really struggling. I mentioned to the responsible elders that it might be a good idea to lift an offering each time and use some of the money to buy enough nShima – maize meal – to feed everyone who attended after the teaching was over. They heartily agreed.

I encouraged them to appoint two trusted men, not related to each other, to count the offering each week and take note of the amount which would be announced to all present. It was also instructive that I insisted that the offering be counted openly on a table at the front where all could see. That was a lesson I had learned previously. In a large assembly I had visited, two men, father and son took the offering into a back room where they counted it, but a careful watch showed that they pocketed a large percentage and only announced the small remaining amount. No wonder some 'elders' were very keen to count the offering.

So it was that at Misaka and Masaiti, my ostensibly anonymous generous contribution to the offering was sufficient to allow the ladies to make a basic meal for all who attended. Could it be that some elderly men and maybe some not-so-elderly men and women attended only because they were hungry and appreciated a good meal? Was I wrong to start such a habit as precedence demanded that it should be continued? I never was quite sure if what I did was right. Was I guilty of instigating a practice that could not be continued after I left? I tried to convince myself that my generosity was more important than the setting of an unsustainable precedent.

Therein lay another lesson. The need to constantly evaluate any innovations I was tempted to introduce as a foreign missionary. Just because we could financially afford to do something didn't necessarily make it right or constructive long-term. We constantly felt the need for divine wisdom.

In conversation with Kelvin Samwata, a Zambian brother and an elder in Chingola Chapel he expressed the opinion that there were some assemblies in and around Mufulira that would benefit from Bible teaching. This was some distance from Kitwe on a not very good road and lay right on the border with the D.R. Congo. He encouraged me to consider visiting there once a month and to facilitate me he accompanied me there on numerous occasions until I got to know the elders there and indeed that they should get to know me. That was very gracious of our brother Kelvin and showed his shepherd heart.

After a while, I continued to visit there alone one Saturday each month and it was a privilege to teach God's Word. Surrounding assemblies were informed and some came so that the fairly large hall was almost full.

But I was about to learn another lesson at Mufulira. A dispute arose among the assemblies throughout Zambia about their Constitution and how the assemblies should be represented legally before the government as was required. Maybe it was more about who should represent them. I took no part in those discussions nor did I express an opinion about the matter, but somehow I presume I was seen as a foreign missionary whom it was assumed would take a certain position. To my amazement, without any consultation with me, the Bible studies were no longer announced to the surrounding assemblies, nor any invitations relayed. So, it was rather disappointing to arrive in Mufulira to discover only a handful of believers who eventually turned up because they had seen my vehicle come through the town centre. I persisted for some months but clearly was no longer welcome nor was the Bible teaching appreciated as at first. So it was that I was obliged to terminate those visits.

I found that both painful and sad that elders should deprive believers of surrounding assemblies the opportunity to listen to the straightforward exposition of Scripture. What annoyed me more was that some capable younger men were learning to love the Scriptures and study them carefully. I also felt that the question-and-answer sessions that followed were of some value. I was saddened that never again was I invited to visit any of those assemblies. It was a painful lesson to learn.

Lesson 3
Margaret Teaching at Amano Christian School

Not long after we settled in Kitwe, there came a request from the relatively recently established Amano Christian School near Chingola. It had both a Primary School and a Secondary School. Somehow news had spread that we were both qualified Secondary teachers and they had a shortage of qualified teachers so both of us would be warmly welcomed to teach at Amano as unpaid volunteers. I politely but firmly refused convinced that it was not what the Lord wanted me to do. My heart was still in teaching the Scriptures and preaching the gospel. However, the plea for a biology teacher was both urgent and pressing as the teacher involved was about to leave to return to the UK. Margaret had taught biology and had many years of experience at secondary level. We prayed and sought the Lord's guidance. It seemed a good match.

Sadly, it was also a considerable distance away from Kitwe on an unpleasantly busy road used by all the heavily loaded copper-mining trucks. However, she accepted the challenge feeling that the Lord's hand was in it but asked that her timetable be reshuffled to minimise the days she would have to travel. So it was that for many years she drove our Toyota pickup the forty or forty-five-minute drive to teach at Amano.

It was such a relief after Luanda that she could now take our vehicle and safely drive by herself to Amano. It was a liberating experience even though both tiresome and at times dangerous because of the density of heavy traffic. She also had to learn how to cope with Zambian policemen.

On her very first day driving alone to Amano Christian School, she overtook a slow truck and was promptly stopped by police. She was told that she had crossed a white line and when she asked where the white line was, she was informed that even though there was no white line painted on the road everyone knew there was a white line there. Can you imagine how Zambian drivers have to watch out for imaginary white lines? Of course, they were very polite and pleasant about it all, but the fine had to be paid. Margaret proceeded to search for the money in her purse only to discover that she hadn't the required amount. Being such considerate men, they asked her how much she had and readily agreed to accept what she had available. It's a learning experience dealing with Zambian policemen when you are a mature white lady by yourself driving a fairly new Toyota pickup. You must be rich or have a rich husband. And in a sense compared to many Zambians living just above the breadline we were relatively wealthy, though we never thought of ourselves as such. She was worried as to what her rich husband would say when she returned home but was suitably relieved when we laughed heartily together at the experience and wondered if it would be advisable for her to never carry any money in her purse in future when driving alone to Amano or simply leave the purse at home. But obviously, there was an urgent need to watch out for unpainted imaginary white lines in future.

Lesson 4
Margaret Teaching Good News Club

There were six English-speaking assemblies that we were familiar with in Kitwe – Kitwe Chapel, Riverside, Nkana East, Cha Cha Cha, Chimwemwe and Ndeke Village - and where we were made welcome to teach the Scriptures or preach the gospel. All were known as 'chapels' in that they predominantly used English in contrast with others which used solely one of the vernacular languages, usually Bemba.

We were not very long settled into Mukuba Village in Kitwe when Margaret got to know a lady, Mrs Annie Sheba, from the neighbouring assembly in Riverside. She had a group of children who came together each Saturday morning for a Good News Club. She would appreciate some help. With Margaret's previous experience in Luanda, we saw it as the Lord opening another door. So it was that for the thirteen years she taught the Good News Club children every Saturday morning we were there with very few exceptions as when malaria struck.

Numbers attending grew steadily. Some of the older ones expressed the desire to come to know Christ as their Saviour so it was a privilege for her to be able to lead them to Christ and then go on teaching them gently each Saturday.

Of course, I was away teaching the Scriptures in Misaka, Masaiti or Mufulira, leaving before Margaret. That worked fine in the dry season but then came the wet season. Margaret had quite a walk to where the children could conveniently meet for Good News Club. It was obvious she needed a small car and the Lord provided the funds that allowed us to buy locally a used automatic Toyota Rav4. It served her well without trouble and was twenty years old when it was sold before we left.

Lesson 5
Regional and Provincial Conferences

In the Zambian provinces where there are numerous assemblies there has been a long tradition of holding regional and provincial conferences. Of course, a conference location in Zambia is different from that in the UK. It is arranged outdoors for a week in the dry season. Numbers are large. The last one at which I was invited to teach at two sessions had more than 9,000 but others would have in excess of 20,000. The provinces where there are most assemblies are North West, Copperbelt and Luapula, a reflection of where most missionaries worked hard for several generations, each building on what had gone before.

The venue is often simply a suitable outdoor space of African bush with adequate shelter from the sun where a large crowd can be accommodated. For some time before the majority arrive, teams of local believers build lots of fences of dried grass separating sleeping areas and lots of latrines and usually an imposing platform for the speakers. Nowadays the luxury of a generator and loudspeaker system is a great help. Whole families arrive in cars, trucks and buses bringing with them their cooking pots, sufficient food for the week and their sleeping mats. A multitude of fires for cooking are lit each evening. The smoke and smell of evening cooking combined with the overarching hum of so many conversations and laughter at a bush conference are unforgettable.

There are times for prayer, teaching sessions by invited speakers and lots of singing. Choirs abound with several performances between the main organized sessions. Africans can sing. Zambians can sing with swaying enthusiasm and in a variety of tribal languages. It is all quite organized. It never ceased to amaze me how well organized it was despite the huge numbers attending.

It is a wonderful time of fellowship that helps to bind believers together, share information and refresh friendships. Young people thoroughly enjoy meeting their own age group and especially some who come from isolated areas. It was probably even more so in earlier days before the ability of so many believers to own cars, not to mention the communication revolution brought about by mobile phones even in outlying villages.

They continue to serve a useful purpose in so far as gifted Bible teachers are invited to teach the Scriptures and clarify sound Biblical doctrine and practice. They can help believers in the continuing ongoing struggle to both contend with wrong teaching and see their way through old errors reappearing in new guises.

There has developed the realisation that time can be allocated to a wide variety of smaller-scale teaching sessions on specific topics given by those gifted to deal with them and are of immense benefit, especially where cultural issues conflict with biblical teaching. Question and answer times work well in smaller groups.

There always remains the challenge of helping young believers see the relevance of sound teaching as they face what seem like modern challenges that their parents never faced. Social media, smartphones and television including the all-pervasive Prosperity Gospel, bring with them spiritual challenges unheard of in a previous generation.

Chapter 10
ANGOLA REVISITED FROM ZAMBIA

Early in the dry season of 2015 while we were in Kitwe, Zambia, it was a pleasant surprise to receive an invitation from a brother in Luena, Fernando Rodrigues, a leading elder among the assemblies in and surrounding Luena and indeed throughout the province of Moxico. The invitation was to participate in a week-long conference of elders from throughout Moxico. I was to teach daily in Portuguese and would be sharing the teaching with Dr Juan Palacio who was living in Luena.

Together with his wife Adriana he was heading up an amazing medical team based in the 'Jesus Salva' (Jesus Saves) large medical clinic already referred to. It has been wonderfully updated, modernised and with additional buildings added since it was first built. In October 2022 the Palacios have had to return to their home country for compelling family medical reasons.

Juan took the first teaching session each morning prior to dashing back to his morning surgery at the clinic where there would be a long queue of patients waiting for him. For me, it was a delight to listen to him teaching God's Word with such ability and passion and with total fluency in Portuguese while I was struggling to regain a degree of fluency.

What a privilege it was to teach those dear men the Scriptures. In one session I believe it was the Holy Spirit that guided me to teach the basics of how to have a daily Quiet Time with God, both reading His Word, praying, and listening to how the Holy Spirit was speaking to each one of us. Sadly, for too many, it seemed like a novel idea. On the other hand, those who were still faithfully doing the Emmaus Bible Correspondence courses were delighted that others should catch the vision of a daily disciplined time with an open Bible, alone with God.

I have overlooked the small matter of how we travelled from Kitwe in Zambia to Luena in Angola. We decided to go by road once we would obtain our Visas to enter Angola. That in itself required patience. Application forms could only be obtained from the Angola Embassy in Lusaka during the morning of specified days. Lusaka is about a minimum of 7 hours' drive from Kitwe. Our application had to be accompanied by a formal 'Letter of Invitation' from Angola and all submitted in person in Lusaka. We waited and waited. Meanwhile the start of the conference in Angola had to be delayed as they waited for our arrival. The Angolan brothers were patient, most understanding and co-operative.

It would be a lengthy trying journey of at least 4 days steady driving of between 8 and 10 hours daily and over roads some of which could scarcely be called proper roads. Our dear sister Ruth Hadley decided that the only way to get us safely through all the Police and Angolan military checkpoints was for her to drive 2 days to meet us at the Zambian/Angolan border post and accompany us back to Saurimo. Likewise on our return journey back to Zambia she would see us safely to the Zambian border post. For her that meant 8 days of tedious hard driving in warm weather and with no air-conditioning in her vehicle. Who else but Ruth would even contemplate doing such a sacrificial thing? Many would think probably more than twice about doing it even on the good roads of the UK.

What made it worse was that in our exchange of emails to coordinate our journeys, she commented that she was having problems with her Land Rover but made no fuss about it. What she didn't tell us was that the chassis of her Land Rover had broken. Now who ever heard of anyone breaking a Land-rover chassis as it seems like the strong chassis of a small truck?

In the goodness of God, Jonathan Singleton undertook to rectify the chassis with what tools and equipment were available to him. Amazingly, he did an excellent strong job. I suspect few mechanics in the UK would ever contemplate such an undertaking even with all the gear available to them.

It was an unforgettable journey. We travelled to Chavuma Mission Station which is about 5 klms from the Angolan border. The late Bob Young kindly accompanied us to the Zambian border. He knew some of the officials and of course, they were all very familiar with the good treatment they and their families had received freely at the Chavuma Mission Hospital. We suspected that that was a factor in making the necessary paperwork go so smoothly before he left us.

We crossed no man's land on a road that most Northern Ireland farmers would never leave in such a deplorable state. Ruth was waiting for us at the Angolan border having actually arrived a short time before us. Speaking fluent Chokwe she made all the officialdom very easy for us. Without her, it would definitely have been a different story. So, we set off ready to cross the first of a series of bridges repaired after being blown up in the war.

Zambian missionaries, including Bob Young and Murray Poidevin, had negotiated with the Angolan authorities to allow them to repair some of the bridges while the Angolan government would repair the remainder. The missionaries worked hard and did an excellent job as they were anxious to regain access to teach and encourage the many assemblies on the Angolan side and at the same time provide them with access to the plentiful supply of goods including Bibles and Christian literature on the Zambian side. The contrast in the level of professionalism in bridge-building was remarkable.

For us, venturing unto some of the bridges built by the Angolan government was a new experience. Access was by means of moveable planks. Each driver had to adjust the width of the space between the planks to align with the front wheels of his vehicle. Then the next vehicle had to do the same. So that's what we had to do. Heaving heavy planks is not for the faint-hearted nor is crossing some of the bridges where some planks were missing or broken.

There was one bridge that was decidedly more tricky than most. Ascending steeply out of deep sand to get onto the bridge was an acquired skill. I could see only the pickup bonnet and the blue sky so had to trust that the vehicle was heading in exactly the right direction. When some African missionaries in remote areas ask people to pray for travelling mercies, they really do mean it.

The prevalence of bare long carefully sharpened steel rods functioning as nails to secure planks tested the quality of most tyres. Is it any wonder that both Ruth and ourselves travelled with at least two good quality spare tyres as well as multiple jerry cans of diesel.

But it was all abundantly worthwhile as there was such a welcome and thirst for the teaching of God's Word and such opportunities to preach the wonderful good news of the gospel.

That trip also allowed us to glimpse some of the amazing work that Ruth had been involved in.

As we talked with Ruth in some of our earlier visits to Saurimo, she highlighted what she identified as the difference between assemblies that were making good progress under the leadership of godly elders in comparison with too many that were led by men who did not have the biblical qualifications of elders. Sadly, some showed little or no sign of true spiritual life which raised doubts as to whether they were truly born again. She was convinced that most if not all of the more spiritually mature elders had benefitted greatly from being boarders at the schools run by a previous generation of missionaries. The impact of the daily teaching of the Scriptures had made a deep lasting impact on the thinking of young students who had professed faith in Christ. By the grace of God and the daily impact of the Holy Spirit, that sound Bible teaching had survived the subsequent atheistic communist brainwashing. Those men lived transformed lives and gained the deep respect of both fellow-believers and their community.

So it was that as conditions improved, she began to plan and prepare to build a school. The only place where that could be done was on mission property not controlled by the government. The nearest suitable area was at Camundambala about 10 kilometres outside Saurimo where there was still not only a mission house but also more than adequate space to contemplate opening a primary school. There would be the freedom to teach the Scriptures daily.

It is hard to imagine just how difficult this was going to be both from all the bureaucracy involved and the sheer scarcity of just about everything. Ruth was a very determined and exceedingly hard-working lady not easily daunted even by a project that would have seemed impossible to many - whether men or women.

At every turn, corrupt and often unsympathetic bureaucrats initially could see no personal benefit in it for them but as the work looked more likely to proceed there began another battle. Ruth's vision was to educate the local village children who had no hope of getting even a basic education. She saw clearly that the benefits of such a school would be many. Village young people who had no hope would have hope, a good basic education, and a future. Moreover, when some boys would trust Christ, as they grew up and matured, they could be a real help both in building up a dead assembly whose 'elders' were a hindrance rather than a spiritual help and the Lord could use them to reach out to surrounding villages with the gospel. She had clear biblical objectives.

Of course, as Saurimo officials in whose jurisdiction Camundambala lay came to see how much superior the level of education was, the commitment of Christian teachers and even the input of Ruth herself, they battled to get their children and family members enrolled. Probably the final straw for many of them was when she not only managed to get the buildings up and Christian teachers employed who were dedicated to their task but after some time added a classroom of computers and began to teach the primary school children how to use them.

Ruth was not a primary school teacher but a secondary school teacher of history and was deeply involved in sports. She was highly competitive and aimed at nothing less than the best.

We were amazed when we visited the school in 2015 to discover that those village primary school children were able to make a PowerPoint presentation and even add music to it. I was flabbergasted. I couldn't do that.

Since Ruth passed away, Brian and Debbie Howden, who have done a sterling work over many years, have seen the benefit of much better educated young men to whom Brian has taught the Scriptures faithfully. These young men are now able to preach and teach with understanding and insight, having been able to read and study the Scriptures for themselves so that now they can teach others acceptably.

All the time Ruth was dedicating considerable sums of money and time building the school classrooms and indeed up until she left Angola, she continued to live very simply in a town centre small bungalow with little space and no luxuries.

While we were visiting the school, she told us an interesting story. Pupils were expected to arrive to start classes at a set time. One day, however, some pupils arrived quite late, so she asked them to explain. An older girl explained that they were held back badly by the slowness of her younger siblings. Ruth then asked them to come to see her at the end of school and she would take them home, which she did. To her amazement they had to walk a long distance, leaving home before dawn and likewise had to walk back home again after school. These were primary school children.

She went to the elders of the village of Kwasamukwenu from which they came and asked them if they would organize a piece of land suitable for a school. They were delighted and over time Ruth funded the construction of a lovely two-classroom primary school and arranged Christian teachers. Not only so but often went there herself for Sunday school on Sunday afternoons. She frequently took young people with her and trained them to do the teaching. She had a vision for teaching and training young people.

On that visit to Angola, Ruth was keen to have Margaret's help in a training session for Sunday school teachers and she arranged it in a classroom at the school in Camundambala. Some of those keen to attend seemed too young to be teaching Sunday School. We suspected that some parents brought their children maybe just in case there might be some handouts and not necessarily written ones.

For one week it was arranged that I should give a Bible Study each evening in one of the Saurimo assemblies specifically timed to allow young men coming from work to attend. It was another excellent opportunity to deal with some very specific topics that were perplexing some of the younger men being increasingly exposed to so-called

Christian tele-evangelists of the Prosperity Gospel variety. What should be made of modern-day African 'prophets' who in reality are closely related to the village witch-doctors of the past? And what about Pentecostal 'speaking in tongues', healing campaigns and the unbiblical aspects of the teachings of the Seventh Day Adventists? It seemed like these were topics needing to be addressed and with the freedom to ask questions. It was obvious that many if not most homes not only had a TV but had access to an immense range of international programmes. There had been many changes in the intervening years since we had left. It was amazing to see so many young people on lightweight mostly Chinese motorbikes including lots of young women dressed in jeans. These bikes were like a swarm of noisy bees at traffic lights.

It was fascinating to see how the thirteen years of political peace after the 2002 death of Jonas Savimbi and the subsequent Peace Accord brought an end to the 30-year civil war but also brought good jobs and financial prosperity. In what had formerly been very basic buildings for local assemblies some had been revamped and updated. Instead of bare cement floors and unpainted grey walls, there were beautiful ceramic tiles. Even air-conditioning had been installed in at least one place and a digital projector as modern as anything I had seen in the UK. The preacher now stood behind a modern transparent glass-like dais instead of the previous solid mahogany variety.

But as in many other countries, increasingly better-educated young couples were now both qualified to hold better-paid jobs. The transformation was really remarkable in a relatively short time.

While I mentioned earlier the challenges of long days of travel from Kitwe in Zambia to Saurimo in Angola, some may wonder where we stayed at night once we crossed the Angolan border. In Zambia that is rarely a problem as fellow missionaries and believers in many towns will gladly offer accommodation and where that may not be feasible there are lodges and guest houses of varying quality.

After a particularly long hard drive from the Angolan border, we arrived at Kavungu where Irene Cardoso has established an amazing base. Her thatched house was built of sun-dried mud blocks but with the passing years, it needed reinforcing buttresses to keep the walls erect and was covered with a tarpaulin as the thatch no longer kept out the rain.

It was such a joyful reunion after so many years. This was the same Irene Cardoso who had helped Margaret in Luanda with Sunday School lessons and other material in Portuguese. What a reunion. She had gone to considerable trouble to have bedrooms very clean, neat and tidy for us and had prepared a meal. She had no electricity or running water. Irene had left a good well-paid job in Luanda to serve the Lord in Kavungu. She was totally dedicated to teaching the Scriptures to ladies and children and to our amazement was preparing to hold a camp for a very large number of women. Earlier there had been one for young people. Like Ruth Hadley she was convinced of the value of a school so had gone ahead with building a school. What an amazing work she was doing to see people saved and built up in their faith by the careful teaching of Scripture. There were a few tough questions that were needing to be discussed from Scripture as she struggled to help elders and others who had only a basic education and few to whom they could turn for additional insight and guidance. Life in the bush without the conveniences of town life is both physically hard and lonely for a single lady. How such ladies need the prayerful support of the Lord's people.

Sadly, it was evident that she was poorly supported financially by Angolan local assemblies though commended to the Lord's work by a Luanda assembly. She was full of initiative, so was working hard to make herself largely self-supporting.

CHAPTER 11
RETIRING TO IRELAND

Lesson 1
Knowing when to leave

We thoroughly enjoyed serving the Lord in Zambia over those 13 years but increasingly we became aware that we were in our 70s and likely to need more medical care as the years passed. Margaret had suffered from asthma for all the years we had known each other, yet in the goodness and grace of God, with the correct medication, it had not caused any serious problems for her. Both of us had our share of malaria, often once a year and also the usual various African bugs or infections but on the whole, the Lord had given us good health with which to serve him. We realised however that we could easily become a burden on our Zambian friends if we had any serious illness. Yes, they cared for us deeply but the local healthcare available had its severe limitations. So prayerfully we made the decision that the time had arrived for us to return to Northern Ireland.

For some years we had already been planning and training others alongside us so that we could leave the work in capable hands.

Lesson 2
Continuing to trust God

So we departed from Ndola airport on the Copperbelt on Tues 27th March 2018 at 15.30 and arrived at Dublin airport at 6.30 am on Wednesday 28th where we were met by my brother Ronnie and his wife Yvonne. The bitterness of the cold wind almost made us wish we were travelling in the opposite direction.

In several ways returning back to Ballymena was more difficult than leaving yet even in that we saw the Lord's hand and timing. For example, when we tried to sell our two-storey house, the sale fell through on several occasions and it took well over a year until it was eventually sold. Waiting is not easy. Looking back, the timing was precise. The nearby bungalow we bought had just come on the market when a buyer completed the purchase of our house. Once again the Lord was teaching us to trust Him even through the vagaries of house selling and buying. That encouraged us to go on trusting His faithfulness and provision in Ireland just as He had done in Portugal, Angola and Zambia.

It was a joy to discover that the local fellowship to which we had returned was thriving and growing in numbers attending and it has been a pleasure to be offered the privilege of teaching God's Word. What was especially heartening to hear was the happy noises of so many young children. African local fellowships tend not to be concerned about a level of noise not customarily acceptable here in the UK so there can be lots of noise and distractions for the audience when the preacher is speaking in village churches. Not untypical was one Sunday when I was preaching in a large hall in Angola with a door at each side near the front. To my surprise, in through one door came a squawking hen closely pursued by a noisy bunch of young lads who were in turn followed by several excited barking dogs. Needless to say, nobody was paying the slightest attention to the preacher until the travelling entertainment exited the opposite door.

Looking back to our years abroad, there were times when we were not quite sure if we were truly in the centre of God's will for us but with the value of hindsight as we reminisce – a noted quality of older folk – time and time again we have seen more clearly that the Lord had been guiding our thinking and had been shaping even our motivation when we were somewhat unsure.

We observe how the Lord preserved us in difficult and sometimes even in physically dangerous situations. What was even more amazing was that despite our many faults and failings the Lord actually used us as His channels so that what was done of lasting value was clearly the work of the Holy Spirit. We were also aware that many people were praying for us. Some may well have been unassuming individual believers in out-of-the-way places. We were also deeply thankful that many were praying for our safety, especially in Angola.

Throughout the years I endeavoured to fulfil at least to some limited extent a biblical principle impressed on me initially by the late William MacDonald, author of many books including 'The Believers Bible Commentary' and the devotional 'One Day at a Time'. He taught me the need to imitate Paul's injunction to his son Timothy in 2 Timothy 2v2 where four generations are mentioned. What a joy and a responsibility it was to be given the opportunity to teach groups of young men who in their turn have been willing to teach others what they had learned. It was a pleasure to try to help to open doors of service for them and so both duplicate my usefulness and make myself redundant. I consider that there is no greater privilege than to invest our lives using all our God-given gifts, abilities and resources to preach the gospel, teach and disciple those who trust Christ and see how God uses them to repeat that process, guided and enabled by the Holy Spirit. Later someone abbreviated the process concisely as the three T's – Teach, Train and Trust.

The Lord also enabled Margaret in her own right to explain the gospel to both children and ladies. Some professed faith. The Lord also entrusted her to teach the Scriptures in many varied situations both to large and small groups whether in a backyard, camps or ladies' Bible teaching conferences.

For both of us while there had to be much flexibility in the methods used there was total inflexibility in the unchanging content of the message of salvation. In the work among students in Kitwe, it was a delight to work together using our combined abilities.

Of course, a moment's reflection also highlights the vital role played by those who prayed for us and the work the Lord had entrusted to us. They were often informed and updated regularly by those likewise dedicating their gifts and abilities in Echoes of Service (Echoes International), Lord's Work Trust, Medical Missionary News, Interlink and Opal Trust. It also never ceased to amaze us how the Lord provided for all our financial needs both personal and for the work without us ever having to ask anyone for financial help.

Another example is as unforgettable as the blue bandages in Luanda. Luanda at that time was classified as one of the most expensive cities in the world to live in. Finances were tight when we were notified of a very generous gift from someone in Australia. We have never visited Australia nor to the best of our knowledge were we known in any local churches in Australia. So how then did someone know of our urgent need? We have no idea, but the Lord knew and guided someone at a critical time to give very generously indeed. We acknowledged the gift but never again heard from them.

So, we owe an immeasurably great debt first to the utter faithfulness of the Lord but also an incalculable debt to all who supported us in such a wide variety of ways. All of what has been accomplished was totally because of the faithfulness of a loving forgiving God using us who are failing flawed servants.

Nonetheless, we wholeheartedly encourage especially young people to offer themselves unreservedly as 'a living sacrifice' Romans 12:1 in enthusiastic service to the living God in response to His 'indescribable gift'. As others have rightly said 'Only one life which will soon be past, only what's done for Christ will last'.

BV - #0136 - 041223 - C14 - 215/143/13 - PB - 9781649603982 - Gloss Lamination